residential Site Valuation & Cost Approach

2nd edition

HONDROS LEARNING™

HONDROS LEARNING™
4140 Executive Parkway
Westerville, Ohio 43081
www.hondroslearning.com

Published 2011. Printed in the United States of America

16 15 14 13 2 3 4 5
978-1-59844-175-8

For more information on, or to purchase, our products, please call 1-866-84LEARN or visit www.hondroslearning.com

Table of Contents

Suggested Syllabus

RESIDENTIAL SITE VALUATION AND COST APPROACH

COURSE DESCRIPTION: This course will help students gain valuable insight and a working knowledge of the various theories and methodologies for performing residential site valuation and developing the cost approach in appraisal practice. Various costing methods will be discussed and applications of the cost approach in residential appraising will be examined. The important distinction between Replacement Cost New and Reproduction Cost New will be discussed, along with an in-depth look at accepted methods for estimating accrued depreciation. An exam is given at the completion of the course in compliance with the qualifying education standards of the Appraiser Qualifications Board.

COURSE OBJECTIVES:

- Demonstrate knowledge of valuation principles vital to site valuation and the cost approach.
- Apply the principle of highest and best use in the valuation of land and site.
- Recognize various types of data that are analyzed and applied in land and site valuation.
- Differentiate the various types of legal descriptions critical to land and site valuation and how to interpret those descriptions.
- Distinguish and calculate various valuation methods for developing opinions of value for land and site valuation.

COURSE TEXTBOOK: *Residential Site Valuation and Cost Approach, 2nd edition,* Hondros Learning™, Copyright © 2011

COURSE CREDIT HOURS: Qualifying education: 15 credit hours. Attendance is mandatory to receive course credit.

INSTRUCTION METHOD: Lecture, illustration, case examples, and workgroup case studies

COURSE OUTLINE with Suggested Time Increments:

DAY 1 (total classroom hours 7.5)

1 hour	Introduction and Overview Chapter 1 Basic Concepts of Land and Value
2.75 hours	Chapter 2 Data Collection and Analysis
1 hour	Lunch
3 hours	Chapter 3 Site Valuation
.75 hours	Chapter 4 Reasons for Separate Site Valuation

DAY 2 (total classroom hours 7.5)

1 hour	Chapter 5 The Cost Approach to Appraisal
2.5 hours	Chapter 6 Calculating Costs
1 hour	Lunch
3 hours	Chapter 7 Depreciation and Final Cost Conclusions
1 hour	Final Examination and Student Surveys

Preface

Hondros Learning™ is proud to present *Residential Site Valuation & Cost Approach, 2nd edition as* part of the market-leading textbook series for appraisal qualifying education. Written specifically to correspond to the most recent Appraisal Qualifications Board's course topic requirements, *Residential Site Valuation & Cost Approach,2nd edition* features **clear writing**, **real-world examples, work problems** and **case studies**, useful **illustrations**, challenging chapter quizzes, and a **glossary** of key terminology, making this text the most up-to-date tool available for achieving mastery of and applying site valuation and the cost approach in appraisal practice.

In addition to following the *AQB content guideline* for qualifying education, all texts in our appraisal series are *affordably priced* and feature a *clear writing style* and *numerous study aids* to assist students with comprehension and application of the material. Concepts range from simple to slightly complex, illustrating the application of the material in various appraisal scenarios. **Key terms** are highlighted and defined throughout and compiled along with other related terms in a useful *glossary.*

Instructor materials are available separately to make using this text in the classroom a seamless experience.

Text Outline

Chapter 1 defines the seven characteristics of real estate including the four value characteristics (demand, utility, scarcity, transferability) that all items must have, as well as the three physical characteristics (uniqueness, immobility, indestructibility) that are unique to real estate. A discussion of public and private restrictions that can affect the value of real property and an explanation of the difference between value, price, and cost and review value principles relevant to site valuation.

Chapter 2 discusses the general data and specific data which must be gathered from various sources. This chapter explains how to identify a site and look at the property specific factors that affect that site.

Chapter 3 focuses on the various methods of site valuation and fully illustrates the sales comparison method and allocation method, as well as the extraction land residual, ground rent capitalization, and subdivision analysis methods.

Chapter 4 offers reviews some of the uses for separate site valuation—highest and best use, developing the cost approach, insurance value, economic life calculations, and property taxes—along with some formulas and examples. The chapter discusses the role of the appraiser, noting Uniform Standards of Professional Appraisal Practice (USPAP) guidelines and obligations and some ways to increase the inherent value of land are explored through assemblage, plottage, and subdivision.

Chapter 5 introduces the cost approach to appraisal, defines it, and then explains when and why it is used. The differences between replacement cost and reproduction cost are explained with important points about each. The principle of substitution is discussed as it relates to the cost approach and the typical buyer. The principle of contribution is also explored along with an explanation of diminishing returns and increasing returns. Finally, this chapter discusses specific reasons and uses for the cost approach.

Chapter 6 examines direct costs, indirect costs, and entrepreneurial considerations for a structure. In addtion, methods of calculting area of a structure are discussed. Most importantly, the chapter offers fully illustrated explanations and examples for the various costing methods.

Chapter 7 discusses concepts of depreciation including important life measurements used in depreciation. The forces of deprection, physical deterioration, and functional and external obsolesence are fully explored along with helpful examples. Various other related depreciation concepts and how to address them are also discussed and illustrated. The chapter concludes with a discussion of final cost approach analysis and reporting.

Exam Prep

Additional appraisal products available from Hondros Learning to help students prepare for the licensing exam include the *Appraisal Review Crammer*™, *3rd edition*—a valuable self-study or classroom exam preparation guide; and *CompuCram*™ *Appraisal Exam Prep Software*.

Contributor Acknowledgements

Hondros Learning™ would like to acknowledge the following contributor for his significant content contributions to this textbook:

Timothy L. Detty

Ohio Certified General Appraiser
Senior Editor—Appraisal Publications
Hondros Learning

Reviewer Acknowledgements

Hondros Learning™ would like to thank the following expert reviewer for his comments and suggestions:

Bruce D. Swearingen

FL State Certified Residential REA
FL State Residential Appraisal Instructor
AQB Certified USPAP Instructor

Basic Concepts of Land and Value

1

Chapter Overview

In order to understand site valuation, there are several definitions and concepts that are important to understand. The seven characteristics of real estate include the four value characteristics (demand, utility, scarcity, transferability) that all items must have, as well as the three physical characteristics (uniqueness, immobility, indestructibility) that are unique to real estate. This chapter will also discuss some public and private restrictions that can affect the value of real property. Finally, we will explain the difference between value, price, and cost, and then review some value principles that are relevant to site valuation.

Key Terms

Anticipation An economic theory that says value is created by the expectation of future benefits (appreciation, tax benefits, income, etc.).

Bundle of Rights All real property rights conferred with ownership including, but not limited to, right of use, right of enjoyment, and right of disposal.

Demand The need or desire for a specific good or service by others.

Market Value Generally, the most probable price that a property should bring in a competitive and open market. There could be many definitions. The appraiser must always identify the definition of market value and cite its source in the report.

Scarcity A physical characteristic of real property that says there is a limited supply of real estate; the perceived supply of a good or service relative to the demand for the item.

Site A parcel of land with enhancements that make it ready for a building or structure.

Substitution A principle that says an informed buyer will not pay more for a property, or a feature in a property than a comparable substitute.

Transferability The ability to freely buy, sell, encumber, or dispose of property in any way the owner sees fit.

Utility The ability of a good or service to satisfy human wants, needs, or desires.

Zoning Government regulation of the uses of property within specified areas.

Site and Value

As the discussion of site valuation begins, let's review some definitions and concepts. A **site** is *a parcel of land with enhancements that make it ready for a building or structure*. These enhancements include on-site improvements, such as utility connections, and off-site improvements, such as road access. The appraiser is interested in the value of the site apart from any buildings or structures on it.

The appraiser must consider many different aspects of site value. There are seven characteristics of real estate: Four value characteristics and three physical characteristics. All of these are important for property value. There are also public and private restrictions on land which can affect its value. Finally, there are **value principles** at work in the marketplace which impact the final market value of real estate. The rest of this chapter will focus on these topics as a prelude to a discussion on calculating site values.

Seven Characteristics of Real Estate

After reviewing the seven characteristics of real estate, note that the four **value characteristics** apply to all products and services—not just land. These must be present in any item for that item to have value. On the other hand, the three **physical characteristics** are unique to real estate. These physical characteristics are what make land inherently valuable. Let's go through the seven characteristics.

Value Characteristics

Value *is the amount of goods or services offered in the marketplace in exchange for something else.* Before anything can have value, the user and other potential users of the property must perceive certain **value characteristics** that must be present. All four of these characteristics must be present and in harmony for the item to achieve maximum value. The four value characteristics are **d**emand, **u**tility, **s**carcity, and **t**ransferability (remember: **D-U-S-T**).

Demand

Demand is *the need or desire for a specific good or service by others*. Demand is an essential ingredient in creating value. Without demand, any amount of supply is meaningless. How many times have you bought something you didn't need or intend to buy at the grocery store, just because it was on sale? Real estate markets can function similarly.

Example

For example, *If a buyer purchases real estate at a low price anticipating that they could hold the property until the market revives and prices go up*, this is called speculation.

The speculator is concerned that even when holding and maintenance costs of the property are considered, they can still make a profit due to acquiring the property at such a low price. Another common example of speculation might simply be the buyer who was not particularly in the market for a property at the present time but found real estate prices to be too good to pass up.

On the other hand, the market cannot raise prices too high, even if there appears to be strong demand. High prices can cause some people to look for alternatives in the marketplace.

Example

> If prices or interest rates become too high, many potential buyers will rent until purchasing becomes more affordable. Or, buyers may simply look for something that fits their needs at a lower price-point.

This is an example of the theory of substitution, which will be discussed later in the chapter.

One final element of demand to consider is the person's ability to pay for the item. Effective purchasing power, also known as **effective demand** or **purchase ability,** means the *prospective buyer has enough disposable income available to satisfy his needs or desires.* A person may want a million dollar home, but if he cannot afford to buy it then that person's demand does not count. In other words, those who create the market for an item must have the means to purchase the item, not just want it.

Utility

Utility is *the ability of a good or service to satisfy human wants, needs, or desires.* Utility is the degree of usefulness to prospective users. For example, there can be demand for housing, but your home must be perceived as useful (e.g., enough bedrooms) to someone interested in buying it for your home to have value to that person. Furthermore, if there is no perceived use for something, then there is no perceived value. This is why the next section of this chapter discusses public and private restrictions on land. For example, government restrictions on the size and placement of buildings may mean that a certain type of building cannot be built on a lot. Any such restrictions can impact the utility and, hence, the value of land. The more restrictions on land, then there are the fewer market participants and, therefore, less demand.

Scarcity

Scarcity is *the perceived supply of a good or service relative to the demand for the item.* If there is an unlimited supply of something, then it is perceived to have little value. Of course, the scarce item must also be useful (i.e., have utility). Scarcity and utility must both be present. Things that are scarce but not useful have little value (e.g., common fossils), just as things that are useful but plentiful have little value (e.g., air and water).

People generally perceive land to be valuable because there is a limited supply of it. This notion of scarcity feeds the anticipation of real estate buyers, because they feel that they are buying property as an investment that will increase in value in the future. Value is also derived from scarcity due to uniqueness—for example, the fact that there is only one of a particular house in a given location. If people really desire a certain home in a certain location then more value may be created.

Transferability

Transferability is *the ability to freely buy, sell, encumber, or dispose of property in any way that the owner sees fit*. Value is derived from the freedom to transfer the title readily from one person to another. The fewer the restrictions on the property then the more perceived value the property has in the marketplace. If there are conditions on title to land which restrict its future transfer, a buyer would likely not pay as much for the land (given that ready substitutes exist in the marketplace). Again, public and private restrictions come into play. If there are any restrictions imposed on transferability, this may decrease the perceived value to potential buyers.

Finally, there is the added requirement that the person receiving the property must have the ability to pay for it. We referred to this earlier as **effective demand** or **purchase ability**. Another way to say this is **effective purchasing power**. Without this, desires and demands go unfulfilled because property cannot be transferred to the person who desires it.

Physical Characteristics

Real estate has three physical characteristics which serve to give land some inherent value. These unique characteristics are not present as a group in other types of property. Only real estate has this combination of physical attributes, and as a result the appraiser must understand how they have the ability to affect value. As we discuss the three physical characteristics of real estate—**uniqueness**, **immobility** and **indestructibility**—note how these characteristics are often intertwined with the four value characteristics.

Uniqueness

Uniqueness is *a physical characteristic of real estate referring to the fact that each piece of land, each building, and each house are said to be a different piece of real estate. No two are exactly the same*. (This is also called **nonhomogeneity**.) Even if two houses or two buildings look the same, they are said to be different because of their location. Since no more land can be created in a given location, this uniqueness leads potential buyers to view land as a scarce commodity. When people want to build in a certain area, they must compete with others for the limited supply of land in that area. Value is derived from this perceived scarcity due to uniqueness.

Immobility

Immobility is *a physical characteristic of real estate referring to the fact that it cannot be moved from one place to another*. This is an equal benefit or detriment to all parcels of real estate in the same general area. This immobility of land helps its value in a good market, since other land cannot be moved in to take away potential customers (as can be done with other products), but it can also hurt land value in a bad market. Consider a general area close to a large body of water or near an industrial site. The site close to a body of water would have more value if you could move it to water frontage. The site close to an industrial plant would have more value if you could move it further away. Immobility is the basis for the three most important things in real estate: Location, Location, and Location. Note that customers are somewhat immobile as well. It is impossible to move a house and land from one city to another where there is a buyer, and usually a person in one city will not buy a house in another city if that person's job cannot move with her.

Indestructibility

Indestructibility is *a physical characteristic of real estate referring to the fact that it cannot be destroyed*. Thus, real estate will always have some minimum value by virtue of its existence. Land is not consumed, nor does it wear out like many other goods. The marketplace or other forces can affect the actual and perceived utility of land. Land always has the potential to be useful, but its usefulness—and hence its value—can change over time.

Public and Private Restrictions

Before we discuss some of the restrictions that can affect real estate value, let's review a few relevant definitions. **Property** is defined as *the right of ownership in a thing, such as the right to use, possess, transfer, or encumber the thing.* Real property generally refers to real estate. Although the terms real property and real estate are often used interchangeably, it is important to know that the Uniform Standards of Professional Appraisal Practice (USPAP) recognizes a technical distinction between them in appraisal theory. Some states recognize this legal distinction but be aware that many states do not.

Real estate refers to *the actual physical land and everything, both natural and man-made, which is attached (or appurtenant) to it*. **Real property**, also called **realty**, refers to not only the physical land and everything attached to it, but also the rights of ownership (**bundle of rights**) in the real estate.

The **bundle of rights** are *all real property rights that are conferred with ownership, including the right of use, the right of enjoyment, and the right of disposal.* Think of the bundle of rights as a bundle of sticks and each stick represents a different right. If one secures the entire bundle of rights then that person is said to be the owner. A person who gives up one or more of their rights is still the owner but with certain restrictions or limitations. In this section, we will discuss some ways that those real property rights can be restricted, voluntarily or involuntarily, by the private sector and by government. These restrictions or limitations may or may not have an impact on real property value.

Public Restrictions

Public restrictions on land use are imposed by the government in a variety of ways and for a variety of reasons. These government restrictions on land can have a serious impact on its value. Governments have four powers: **P**olice power, **e**minent domain, **t**axation, and **e**scheat. (Remember: **P-E-T-E.**)

Police Power

Police power is *the constitutional power of state (and local) governments to enact and enforce laws that protect the public's health, safety, morals, and general welfare*. From an appraisal standpoint, the most important restrictions that government can place on land come from its police power. Police power can take the form of **land use controls** (primarily **zoning laws** and **building codes**) and **environmental protection laws**.

- **Zoning laws** *are local ordinances dividing a city, county, etc. into zones, allowing different types of land use in different areas*. Zoning and other laws restricting land usage (e.g., building codes) are passed to protect the health, safety, and welfare of the community. Land use controls impact real estate since they may limit development, thus affecting property values. Land may be more valuable with an office building instead of a house, but zoning laws may not permit that land usage. Other zoning ordinances may also restrict how and where the building may be constructed on the property, minimum lot size and building height limits, setback and side yard rules, permitted building density, off-street parking requirements, and other things which a local government may feel are necessary. Exceptions to zoning laws are possible but often not easily obtained.

- **Building codes** *set construction standards, which require builders to use particular methods and materials*. A local government usually has many building codes, such as fire codes, plumbing codes, electrical codes, and etc. In most states, minimum building standards are set by state law, but a local government can require more. The appraiser must consider whether or not the proposed highest and best use for the property can be economically done, given the applicable building code regulations that must be complied with.

Example

Putting a large commercial building on a property located in a flood plain may require additional foundation support or superstructure reinforcement to keep the structure in line with state and local building codes. This will add to development costs.

Building codes vary substantially depending on location. For example, building codes in California will be more stringent due to potential earthquakes than building codes in areas that are not prone to earthquakes. Hurricane prone areas and heavy snow areas are other examples of areas with possible stringent codes.

- **Environmental protection laws** are land use controls at state and federal levels increasing as a means to protect the environment. Regulations can involve blocking or restricting the use of land where there are environmental concerns. Sometimes this conflicts with land owners' usage of land. For example, land cannot be used for a hazardous waste site (or some industrial uses) without government approval. The government also controls land use in protecting wildlife, endangered species and wetlands. Federal agencies may deem land a safe haven or a protected area that cannot be developed.

Eminent Domain

Eminent domain is *the government's constitutional power (right) to take (or appropriate or condemn) private property for public use, as long as the owner is paid just compensation.* Eminent domain affects real estate because of government involvement in fair market pricing, and by making adjacent land more or less valuable depending on a proposed use (e.g., freeway interchange versus a landfill). (Remember: eminent domain is the "right"; condemnation is the "action.")

Taxation

Taxation is *the process of government levying a charge upon people or things.* This is specifically talking about property taxes (called *ad valorem* taxes). Low taxes might encourage real estate activity in a certain area, whereas high taxes could have the opposite effect. **Special assessments** (do not confuse this with "special assessments that are levied by homeowners associations [HOA]). are *taxes levied only against properties that benefit from a public improvement* (e.g., new sewer line). Although the property benefits from this, the resulting higher taxes could cause buyers to shun the property in favor of substitutes that do not have to pay the tax. All of these have the potential to affect the value of real estate in the marketplace.

Escheat

Escheat is when *property reverts to the state after a person dies without leaving a valid will and without heirs*. (Property also reverts to the state after abandonment.) The thinking goes that since the rights of property ownership are derived from the government, those rights should revert to the state if they are not assigned to someone else by the owner, or if there are no heirs. Government actions can affect the value of real estate in an area by disposing of the land or utilizing it in certain ways that are beneficial or detrimental to other properties in the area.

Private Restrictions

A former owner of developer can impose private restrictions on land. These restrictions may or may not have an impact on land value, depending on their purpose and the severity of these restrictions. The two main types of private restrictions that this unit will focus on are **deed restrictions** and **easements**.

Deed Restrictions

Deed restrictions are *limitations on real property use, imposed by a former owner through language included in the deed*. These may also be called **restrictive covenants**, especially if they are recorded in a later document. Deed restrictions and restrictive covenants that are recorded "run with the land" and are thus enforceable against future owners of the property. Note, however, that deed restrictions and restrictive covenants must "touch and concern" the land in order to be legal and binding on future transfers. Usually, these restrictions make a new owner promise not to use property in a particular way.

Example

> Suppose Fast Food Enterprise decides to build a new location a few doors down from an old location, instead of remodeling the existing restaurant. When they go to sell the old land, they would likely include a deed restriction that would prohibit another fast food restaurant from using that location to compete against them. Depending on the dynamics of the marketplace, this type of restriction may or may not have a negative impact on value.

A declaration of **covenants, conditions, and restrictions (CC&R)** is often placed in the deed by the original subdivider of land, although CC&Rs can also be added later. The purpose of CC&Rs is to keep the subdivision attractive and protect the market value of homes. Examples include deed restrictions, such as setting a minimum size of house that must be built on the land or prohibitions against certain types of fences. These types of deed restrictions can have a positive impact on value because they promote conformity in the neighborhood. Severe restrictions could hurt property value, but this is usually not the case with subdivision CC&Rs.

Easements

An **easement** is a *right to use another person's real property for a particular purpose.* Easements can be public (e.g., road expansion) or private (e.g., access to a landlocked parcel). It is important to understand that easements restrict how a parcel of land may be used because usually a structure cannot be put on an easement. The easement creates limited rights to the easement holder.

Easements can be put into a deed before a transfer of property occurs or created separately as an agreement between the parties. A recorded easement (either in a deed or as a separate document) gives notice to third parties and usually causes the easement to transfer with the property. When put into a deed, the easement becomes a restriction, and it often grants the previous owner or other parties an easement for access across the piece of land being transferred. An easement that grants access is referred to as a **right-of-way (ROW)**. Often the government holds a ROW easement across the front of land for future road widening. In either case, easements may have a negative impact on value if they severely limit the buildable area of a site. In some states, a parcel of land cannot be "landlocked," and an adjacent landowner can be forced to provide an easement which can impact value.

Value Principles

As we begin to look at value, let's make a few distinctions clear. **Value** is *the amount of goods or services offered in the marketplace in exchange for something else*, but value does not always equal price. **Price** is *what a particular person is willing to pay for something*. Value is what a typical person would pay for something; price is what one person paid. Of course, both value and price may have nothing to do with what the property actually cost to build. **Cost** is the dollars needed to develop, produce, or build something. (There are many cost factors which must be considered.)

Market value is *the most probable price which a property should bring in a competitive and open market.* Market value is what property is expected to sell for in a typical arm's length transaction. An **arm's length transaction** means *the transaction occurred under typical conditions in the marketplace where each of the parties were acting in his or her own best interests.* Those typical conditions are:

1. The buyer paid cash for the property at closing or obtained a conventional mortgage through a lender so as to pay the seller the agreed upon price at closing.
2. The seller did not grant any unusual payment concessions, such as owner financing or other payment terms.
3. The buyer and seller are not related in any way.
4. The buyer and seller are both acting in their own best interests.
5. The buyer and seller are not acting out of undue haste or duress.
6. The buyer and seller are both reasonably informed about all aspects of the property, its potential uses, market value, and market conditions.
7. The property has been available on the market for a reasonable period of time. (There is not always a set time for this, and it may vary by market conditions.)

As these typical market participants—buyers and sellers—act in their own best interests, they are still guided by the same value principles and other factors that influence value. As such, it is important to understand these factors in order for the appraiser to correctly interpret data. Let's look at the value principles that are most relevant to site valuation.

Anticipation

Anticipation *is an economic theory that says value is created by the expectation of future benefits*. These future benefits that are the motivation for buying real estate include appreciation, tax benefits, and income. Appreciation is almost a universal motivation. While there is no guarantee that property will go up in value, few people (if any) will buy property with the hope or desire that its value will drop. Tax benefits serve as an additional motivating factor as well. Tax shelter benefits have been reduced significantly for many investors, but sometimes there are still tax incentives available for businesses that bring jobs to an area. And for people buying a personal residence, the mortgage interest deduction is an anticipated benefit. Finally, for income properties, there is the anticipation of future income that motivates many investment purchases. Here the investor looks at the future expected income stream as well as the expected future resale value. Be aware that anticipation may also cause investors to buy and hold land for future development.

Balance

Balance is *the right mix of capital, entrepreneurship/management, labor, and land that results in the best return on investment from land* (remember: **C-E-L-L**). In other words, when considering all of these factors just mentioned, which combination of these factors results in the best return on investment from the land. This determines the land's maximum productivity, and, hence, maximizes the value of the site. When these four agents of production (C-E-L-L) are in optimal balance, then the property is at its highest and best use. Balance can also come into play with regard to the economic situation in an area. For example, if there are lots of residential properties in an area, but little commercial development, then land that can be developed for shopping or restaurants would be more attractive as an investment to fill the current imbalance in the area. This can be understood by examining the development pattern of most areas. First, land is used for industrial or large commercial uses to create jobs in an area. Next, land is used for residential purposes so that people can live near those jobs. Finally, land is used for light commercial uses (e.g., store, restaurants, etc.) to serve those people. Note that once the area has enough of a certain type of property usage (e.g., commercial), then values will likely fall for any additional land in that usage category.

Change

Change is a principle affecting value which says that all factors which influence real estate—**p**hysical, **e**conomic, **g**overnmental, **s**ocial (P-E-G-S)—are constantly changing, and thus property value itself is subject to constant change as well. These factors will be discussed in the next chapter. For now, understand that no conditions in any market remain constant forever, and these changes may also cause site value to change. This is why an appraisal is only valid as of its effective date (the date for which value was established). The changes may be subtle or drastic, but it is the appraiser's responsibility to ensure that all changeable factors affecting property value are taken into account in an appraisal.

Competition

Competition is *when two or more parties, properties, etc., are trying to obtain the same thing.* When we talk about competition affecting property value, we are simply acknowledging that properties compete with one another in the marketplace for the attention of buyers. An informed buyer will consider other available properties before making a decision, so a property that purports to have a higher value must have something to distinguish it from other competing properties in the marketplace. Without something to justify a higher value (e.g., the last lot in an area) then the upper limit of value for a property is likely to be no higher than the highest competing property in the area. This is also the **theory of substitution** at work.

Externalities

Externalities are any *event, item, etc., outside the boundaries of a property.* There are many factors outside a property that can affect its value. The main physical externalities that affect value include:

- Neighborhood
- Nuisances
- Environmental hazards

These can affect an entire area or just one property. The appraiser's job is to formulate an opinion as to their effect on value. If a specific externality hurts the value of a property, this should be explained in the appraisal report so that users of the report can follow the appraiser's reasoning.

Substitution

Substitution says that *an informed buyer will not pay more for a property, or a feature in a property, than a comparable substitute*. Although, each property is said to be unique, there is a point beyond which a buyer will not go for a particular property. Even when a buyer really likes a property, if the price is too high then the buyer will seek out a ready substitute in the market. Of course, no one really knows what price point is too high until a person tries to sell property for too much and no one buys it. Furthermore, investors buying a property for a future income stream are usually more price-sensitive than a home buyer interested in a nice place to live. Theoretically, to an investor, income from one property is as good as another. If the price is too high, the investor will seek another substitute investment.

Supply and Demand

The law of **supply and demand** says that for *all products, goods, and services when supply exceeds demand, prices will fall, and when demand exceeds supply, prices will rise*. Real estate markets also respond to the laws of supply and demand, but there is a lag time that exists for market forces to respond. This lag time is the result of the time it takes for real estate to be bought, sold, or developed. If developers see a need for housing, it takes time for them to build houses; and when they see that there is no longer a need for housing, they often have some houses started which still must be finished. The exact lag time for market forces to respond to supply and demand situations depends on the different property types and uses in an area.

SUMMARY

1. A **site** is a parcel of land with enhancements that make it ready for a building or structure. **Enhancements** can be on-site improvements (e.g., utility connections) or off-site improvements (e.g., road access). An appraiser must consider the value of the site separately from any buildings or structures.
2. **Value** is amount of goods or services offered in marketplace in exchange for something. Seven characteristics of real estate consist of four value and three physical. Maximizing value requires four value characteristics: DUST—**d**emand, **u**tility, **s**carcity, and **t**ransferability; plus, the three physical characteristics which are immobility, indestructibility, and uniqueness. Buyers must want a site, feel it is useful to satisfy needs, perceive limited supply, and be free to transfer the site later. To have value, **scarcity** must be coupled with utility. Without demand, supply is meaningless, but a person must also have ability to purchase (effective demand).
3. **Property** is the right of ownership in a thing, such as the right to use, possess, transfer or encumber it. **Real estate** is the actual physical land and all things attached (appurtenant) to it. **Real property** is land and **rights of ownership** in real estate (real property = realty). **Bundle of rights** are all real property rights conferred with ownership (right of use, right of enjoyment, right of disposal). **Owner** is one who secures entire bundle of rights.
4. Public and private restrictions on land can affect value. Public restrictions include four powers of government: **P**olice power, **e**minent domain, **t**axation, and **e**scheat (P-E-T-E). Government restrictions via police power that can impact land value include zoning, building codes, and environmental laws. Private restrictions on ownership are deed restrictions (restrictive covenants, CC&Rs) and easements and are often used by original subdivider but can be added later and must touch and concern the land to be legal (e.g., minimum house size).
5. Value and price are not always equal. **Value** is what a typical person would pay. **Price** is what one specific person paid. **Cost** is dollars needed to build. **Market Value** is the most probable price. Typical transaction is equal to an **arm's length transaction** which is when a transaction occurs under typical conditions in the marketplace where all parties are acting in their own best interests. Typical conditions are: 1. Paid cash or mortgage thru lender, 2. No owner financing or unusual payment terms, 3. Buyer and seller not related, 4. Buyer and seller acting in own best interests, 5. No undue haste or duress, 6. Parties are reasonably informed about property and market, and 7. Property has been on market for reasonable period of time.
6. Value principles are: **Anticipation** which is when value is created by expectation of future benefits—appreciation, tax benefits, income; **balance** which is the best return on an investment that occurs with the right mix of **c**apital, **e**ntrepreneurship, **l**abor, and **l**and—CELL; **change** is all factors affecting value are changing; **competition** is two or more buyers or properties that compete in the marketplace; **externalities** is anything outside a property that affects value; **substitution** is when an informed buyer will not pay more than comparable substitute; **supply and demand** is if supply exceeds demand then prices fall and if demand exceeds supply then prices rise.

QUIZ

1. ***A parcel of land with on-site improvements (e.g., utilities) is best referred to as***
   a. a plate.
   b. raw land.
   c. a site.
   d. a structure.

2. ***What are the value characteristics property must have in harmony to maximize value?***
   a. demand, utility, scarcity, transferability
   b. right of use, enjoyment, and disposal
   c. utility and scarcity, coupled with a lack of purchasing power
   d. uniqueness, immobility, indestructibility

3. ***An appraiser is inspecting a site which is in close proximity to a major intersection. Due to the proximity, the jurisdiction will not allow a curb cut for a driveway. Which characteristic of value is affected by the prohibition?***
   a. change
   b. conformity
   c, location
   d. utility

4. ***The bundle of rights that are conferred with ownership of real property include***
   a. environmental protection laws.
   b. restrictions.
   c. right of enjoyment.
   d. zoning.

5. ***Which is not a police power of government?***
   a. building codes
   b. environmental laws
   c. restrictive covenants
   d. zoning laws

6. ***The government's constitutional power to take private property for public use as long as the government pays the owner just compensation is called***
   a. condemnation.
   b. confiscation.
   c. eminent domain.
   d. immediate possession.

7. ***Private restrictions on land can include all of the following, EXCEPT***
   a. deed restrictions.
   b. easements.
   c. eminent domain.
   d. restrictive convenants.

8. ***An easement that grants access to property is referred to as***
   a. DHA.
   b. FHA.
   c. POW.
   d. ROW.

9. ***The amount that one particular person paid for property is its***
   a. cost.
   b. market value.
   c. price.
   d. value.

10. ***Prior to any adjustments, which is most likely to NOT represent an arm's length transaction?***
    a. The buyer and seller are not related.
    b. The buyer paid closing costs customary in the market.
    c. The property has been available for on the market for a reasonable amount of time.
    d. The seller carried a large second mortgage at a below market interest rate.

11. ***If a new business is getting a tax break by building in a certain location, which value principle is at work?***
    a. anticipation
    b. balance
    c. substitution
    d. supply and demand

12. ***A jurisdiction has just passed a new law which limits the size of a residential building lot. Which police power is this is an example of?***
    a. building codes
    b. physical forces
    c. regression
    d. zoning ordinances

2

Data Collection and Analysis

Chapter Overview

The collection and analysis of appraisal data is an important step for site valuation. This chapter discusses the general data and specific data which must be gathered from various sources. The data can help the appraiser identify the market area where the site competes and define neighborhood boundaries. This chapter also explains how to identify a site and look at the property specific factors that affect that site. These include physical, economic, governmental, and social factors. Finally, this chapter summarizes highest and best use analysis for a site.

Key Terms

District The narrowest of definitions of a market area. A district is an area consisting of one particular land use, such as multi-family residential, commercial, industrial, etc.

Gentrification The process of rapid revitalization of properties in a neighborhood, which causes current residents to be displaced.

Government Survey System A legal description for land, referencing principal meridians and base lines designated throughout the country. Also called **Rectangular Survey** or **Township System**.

Highest and Best Use The most profitable, legally permitted, economically feasible, and physically possible use of a property.

Linkages The time-distance relationship to services between properties and services that people in the market rely on such as schools, employment, and shopping, etc. Also considered is transportation available and how affordable the transportation is. The concept could also relate to the efficiency of how products might be transported as well.

Location Survey The process of verifying that an improvement properly sits within the boundaries of the property and there are no encroachments from neighboring land onto the subject property.

Lot and Block A legal description used for platted property. The description states only the property's lot and block number in a particular subdivision; to find out the exact location of property boundaries, the plat map for that subdivision must be consulted at the county recorder's office.

(continued on page 15)

Appraisal Data

Site valuation, like all appraisal work, depends on collection and interpretation of data. In a market value assignment, this allows the appraiser to form an opinion of value based on what a typical person would pay for property as determined by examining the marketplace. Data collection is an important part of the appraisal process. Just as important is verification and analysis of the data. In fact, verification is one of the most important aspects of an appraisal. All data collected should first be verified for relevancy, accuracy, and reliability. Furthermore, the appraiser must update some data regularly to ensure that it is the most current available.

A thorough appraiser will have a system to keep track of various sources he uses, such as online Internet website bookmarks, filing cabinets of sources, notebooks of data, etc. In a neighborhood data file, an appraiser might have census tracts on file along with a list of other information. This databank would include such things as neighborhood boundaries, zoning, and price range of property in the area.

Technology Databases

Technology can efficiently help the appraiser perform routine tasks, compile data, process paperwork, and write reports. They also provide access to online information and databases as a means of collecting and verifying information. In addition, most public records and other public information can be obtained online and still more information on building costs, economic trends, and real estate in general can be found on the internet. Plus, multiple listing services (MLS) from local real estate boards and other third party information services are available online in most areas.

Even with all of this technology, however, the responsibility for credibility of the data rests with the appraiser. Nothing can surpass the appraiser's own knowledge, experience, records, direct contacts, and personal inspection when sifting through various data sources. These data sources can be **general data** or **specific data**.

General data usually cover forces that affect a property's value but are not directly related to a particular property. General data *encompass all information that affects a particular area or region*. This includes social trends and physical features, as well as information relevant to business and the housing market nationally and locally (e.g., economic trends and government policies). All of the four great forces that affect real estate come into play when looking at general data.

Specific data *cover all information relevant to the subject property itself.* Specific data include such things as features of the site and improvements, as well as collected information for comparative purposes (e.g., comparable sales, cost data, income information). When we examine specific data in an upcoming section, there is a distinction made between subject data and comparative data.

General Data Resources

General data resources cover some of the broad forces that affect value: **P**hysical, **e**conomic, **g**overnmental, and **s**ocial (remember: P-E-G-S). Appraisers must stay current on interest rate trends on a national level and must be up on business conditions affecting the economic base of an area. Changes in federal laws are as important as changes in local laws—particularly zoning. Demographic changes, population shifts, and buyer tastes on the national and local levels are all important. Physical and environmental changes and trends also come into play.

General data resources can be subdivided into sources on the national and local levels. Depending on the assignment, further clarification may be needed on a regional, state-wide, or city level. Appraisers must have ready access to general data information in a given region or area. An appraiser who is active in a particular area may not have to do this general assessment every time an appraisal is done. Rather, an appraiser regularly checks general data resources and updates files which contain facts and information relevant to the real estate markets where she does appraisals most often. Typically, appraisers use general data to spot trends such as:

- Is the economy (or perceptions of it) generally favorable and thus conducive to more activity in the real estate market?
- What about interest rate trends?
- Are there new government regulations coming that might impact real estate?
- What demographic changes are taking place?
- Is the population growing or declining in the city/region?

On the local level, the appraiser may need additional general information covering the economy and government, such as:

- Is a local business looking to expand and add more jobs, or are layoffs coming?
- How stable is the economic base and is it dependent on one primary industry, or are many sectors contributing to stability?
- Are there any growth plans for the city, and if so in what direction?
- Are there any zoning changes that are likely to take place in the near future?

An important component in many assignments regarding site analysis is identification of **linkages,** and how this factor influences value. Linkage is the *time-distance relationship to services between properties and services that people in the market rely on such as schools, employment, and shopping, etc. Also considered is the availability and affordability of transportation.* The concept could also relate to the efficiency of how products might be transported as well.

General data sources used for watching these trends are typically government records, public records and filings, magazines, newsletters, trade publications, and other sources the appraiser relies on because of timeliness and accuracy.

Key Terms

Market Area The broadest of all terms identifying the boundaries of a particular area. Market area takes into account the land uses and characteristics of typical market participants within the defined area.

Metes and Bounds System A legal description that starts at an easily identifiable point of beginning (POB), then describes the property's boundaries in terms of courses (compass directions) and distances, ultimately returning to the POB.

Neighborhood A compilation of complementary land uses.

Plat A detailed survey map of a subdivision or other grouped lots of land, recorded in the county where the land is located. Subdivided property is often called **Platted Property**. Also called **Plat Map**.

GENERAL DATA RESOURCES DATA BANK		
Government Repositories	**Professional Repositories**	**Other Resources**
Government Census Data	Trade Publications or Newsletters	Magazines, Newspapers
Government Publications	Professional Magazines, Journals	Maps And Reports
Government Records	Realtor® Boards, Publications	Lenders, Mortgage Companies.
Courthouse and Registrars	Multiple Listing Services	Property Mgrs, Rental Companies
Public Records and Filings	Computer Databases & Internet	Moving and Storage Companies
U.S. Dept of Commerce or Local Chamber of Commerce	Home Builder Associations Or Other Professional Associations	Employment Agencies or Labor Groups
Planning, Highway, County Commissioners' Offices	Accountants, Lawyers, Engineers, Business People	Builders, Contractors, Architects
Fha or Other Gov't Agencies	Specialized Research Companies	Colleagues and Contacts

Note: These data lists are not all inclusive. Other data sources may also be used. Much of this information is available online from various websites on the Internet.

Specific Data Resources

Specific data resources can be subdivided into sources that provide:

- Specific data or information about the subject property.
- Sources that provide specific data.
- Information for comparative purposes.

The appraiser is interested in specific facts, numbers, and data that are relevant to the property being appraised. Some research can be done to obtain this information using courthouse records, computerized databases, and/or the Internet as the starting point for compiling information on the subject property. An appraiser always checks the accuracy of information. One of the most important ways to obtain accurate and reliable data is by doing a personal inspection of the subject property.

Specific data about the subject property includes information on a subject's site and improvements. Specific data for comparative purposes requires that data be obtained for each of the appraisal methods, which are sales, comparison, cost, and income. Sources that provide specific data or information for comparative analysis purposes will vary depending on the valuation methods being developed in the assignment. Like the personal inspection of the subject property noted above, the most reliable data obtained for comparative purposes is also of a personal nature. The appraiser's files of other appraisals, buyers, and sellers, as well as real estate agents or other professionals involved in real estate transactions are often the appraiser's best source of information. It is hard to know the reasons, motivations, concessions, or other special circumstances that may have influenced a transaction, unless one talks to the parties involved. In fact, sometimes this is the only way to make sure that a sale was an arm's length transaction, and there was no undue pressure on either of the parties to act.

Unlike general data resources, an appraiser reviews specific data for relevancy in each appraisal assignment. All data should be the most recent and relevant data available. As you review the chart below, note that there is some overlap between the different types of specific data and with general data resources.

SPECIFIC DATA RESOURCES DATA BANK		
PROPERTY SPECIFIC:		
Personal Inspection	County Records: Deed, Mortgage, Tax	Multiple Listing Services
Buyer, Seller, Broker, Agent	Computer Databases and Internet	Published, Recorded Info
COMPARATIVE DATA:		
Sales Comparison Data	**Cost Approach Data**	**Income/Expense Data**
Personal Inspection (Condition)	Personal Inspection (Depreciation)	Personal Inspection (Vacancy)
Buyer, Seller, Broker, Agent	Cost Manuals (Books, Elec., Online)	Seller, Broker, Agent
County Records: Deed, Mortgage, Tax	Supply Houses, Labor Pools	Property Managers, Rental Companies
Multiple Listing Services	Architects, Contractors, Engineers	Accountants, Other Professionals
Computer Databases	Computer Databases and Internet	Financial Statements
Published, Recorded Info	Professional Magazines, Journals, Organizations	Professional Journals, Organizations

Note: These data lists are not all inclusive. Other data sources may also be used. Much of this information is available online from various websites on the Internet.

Defining Real Estate Markets

To arrive at the most credible value opinion possible, the appraiser must examine the specific **market area** where properties and buyers are competing.

- A market area is the broadest of all terms identifying the boundaries of a particular area. When describing a market area, the appraiser is providing an account of the land uses and characteristic of typical market participants within the defined area.

A market area can be interpreted in various ways. Market areas can be delineated by the following:

- Property use (residential or commercial)
- Property type (single family or multi-family units)
- Government services (school districts or tax districts)
- Environmental factors (resort property or proximity to hazards)

In fact, one way to delineate the market is to examine some of the value principles from the first chapter. Properties that share the same externalities or share the same demographics may be considered part of the same market. Furthermore, any property that a buyer would readily perceive as a substitute can be put into a specific real estate market. The appraiser does his best to continue to break down the market until it is as defined and focused as practical.

- As the appraiser begins defining the real estate market, some market divisions are easy and obvious. Since location is an important aspect of property value, it is natural to use geographic barriers as one way to define a market area. People who are interested in property in one geographic area generally limit themselves to that area. This delineation can continue right down to the neighborhood level. That is why comparable sales used in the appraisal process should come from the same neighborhood. The delineation of the market along neighborhood boundaries serves as a useful way to define the market, ensuring that activity within that market area will produce the most accurate reflection of market value there.

Neighborhoods

A **neighborhood** is a *compilation or a group of complimentary uses*. A neighborhood is simply a small part of a larger community or market area. When describing a neighborhood, the appraiser is looking at all of the uses, even though varied, which create the overall environment. The complementary uses could be a mix of residential, commercial, and service, as well as other amenities. The neighborhood could share physical characteristics (e.g., similar style or age) or physical boundaries (e.g., natural boundaries, such as a river, or artificial boundaries, such as a highway). But neighborhoods can also be defined by other characteristics. Properties that have similar uses or zoning, price ranges or income levels, or properties that share shopping, social, civic or recreational facilities may all be considered as part of the same neighborhood. In fact, almost any distinguishing characteristic of properties or market areas can be used to define a neighborhood—except those things prohibited by fair housing laws (i.e., race, color, religion, etc.).

Time and effort must be taken to ensure that the appraiser correctly defines the neighborhood, so the market data chosen for the appraisal will reflect a relevant comparison of value. In fact in some appraisals, defining the neighborhood can lead to a complex analysis.

Neighborhood Boundaries

First, the appraiser will often define a neighborhood by looking at the natural and artificial geographic boundaries of an area. Natural boundaries include the obvious rivers and lakes but also the less obvious parks, mountains, or valleys. Artificial boundaries include such man-made things as streets, highways and railroads, and may also be drawn along school, zoning, or political districts.

Next, the appraiser should observe the area to test these boundaries. This observation should look at the preliminary area that the appraiser has identified to observe if there are perceptible changes in neighborhood characteristics at any of the physical boundaries that the appraiser defined. During observation, the appraiser is also looking for similarity of land usage and types of improvements, as well as consistency of building style, landscaping, and even maintenance or upkeep as a means of confirming neighborhood boundaries.

Finally, the appraiser should test her conclusion of neighborhood boundaries by comparing the social and economic characteristics of the area to make sure that these are consistent within the defined neighborhood. Census data or other data on age, occupation, income level, etc., should be gathered and compared as a final step in confirming that the appraiser has appropriately defined the neighborhood.

Districts

A **district** is *an area consisting of particular land use, such as muiti-family, residential, commercial, and industrial, etc*. The term district is the narrowest delineation of within a market area. When an appraiser analyzes and describes a market area there could be more than one neighborhood or district included in the process. For example, a metropolitan downtown area could have a specific entertainment district consisting of numerous restaurants, bars, and theaters. Obviously, areas zoned and used for residential use would also be defined as a district.

Life Cycles

If a market area or neighborhood has been correctly defined, there is usually little in the way of future changes or alterations to its boundaries. Occasionally a new section may be added to a neighborhood, or a change in a road may cut off some houses that were once considered part of a neighborhood. But a neighborhood that is properly defined—taking into account not only physical boundaries but also style, age, usage, and income levels—will likely continue to age together. In fact, all properties in a market area, neighborhood, or district go through their life cycle together. The four phases are **growth**, **stability/equilibrium**, **decline,** and **revitalization**.

Growth

Growth is *the first stage a neighborhood goes through, when property values tend to rise as development activity begins and continues*. Buyers fuel this growth by continuing to purchase property in the area. This demand equals acceptance of the area and prices being charged and causes the area to grow into maturity.

Stability/Equilibrium

Stability or **equilibrium** is *the second stage that a neighborhood goes through, when property values are at their highest level and the area is built up to the point where there is little, if any, vacant property*. Demand typically remains high, as buyers continue to prefer this neighborhood as it enters a mature stage. Prices will rarely drop during this period as the real estate market is near equilibrium. Stability and maturity are characteristic of the equilibrium stage in a neighborhood's life cycle.

Decline

Decline is *the third stage that a neighborhood goes through, when property values begin to fall as demand falls*. Decline in a neighborhood is typically observable through deterioration or decay. This in turn leads to the area becoming even less desirable, and the cycle feeds upon itself. A less desirable area where properties exhibit deferred maintenance translates into lower prices, and lower prices mean that lower-income residents with less money to spend on repairs will be attracted to the homes. As values decline, the problem is compounded by conversion of some properties to rental units (where upkeep is often not as meticulous as by owner-occupants) or to commercial uses. This may, in turn, accelerate the decline.

Revitalization

Revitalization is *the final stage a neighborhood goes through, when property values begin to rise again as demand increases, resulting in increased renovation and rehabilitation.* After a complete revitalization stage, the neighborhood can return to a stability/equilibrium stage, and the cycle will begin again. Revitalization occurs when properties are seen as attractive again for their location, architectural features, or maybe even price. Whatever the reason, people begin to spend money to fix up these homes, and they become desirable again. Revitalization is generally a slow process. *The process of rapid revitalization of properties where current residents are displaced* is called **gentrification**. While this benefits the neighborhood, it can create problems for tenants who are forced from the area due to higher rents.

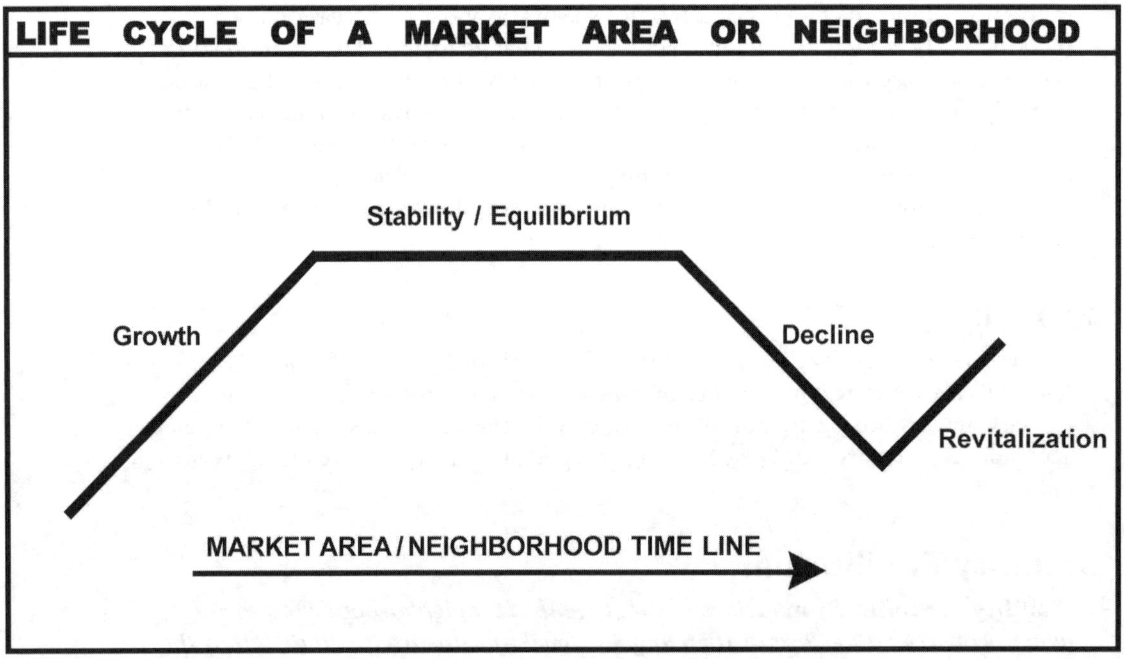

Life cycle of a market area / neighborhood / district.

Separate Site Analysis

Once the market area has been identified and the appropriate data gathered, the next step is collecting and analyzing data for the site. The site is analyzed as a separate entity apart from any buildings or improvements that are on the land because the site might be worth more if it were put to another use. Analysis should initially start with determining if the site is considered a surplus or an excess site.

Surplus site is *the portion over and above what is necessary for the highest and best use of the subject property, and does not have a stand-alone highest and best use*. Surplus land is not needed to expand the subject improvements or that of an adjoining property. In other words, it does not have sales potential and value contribution is minimal.

For example, consider a house that is built across two lots accommodating a larger yard area. If the extra yard cannot be legally divided or it is not needed, or could significantly contribute to the expansion of the current improvements, the extra yard is likely surplus and would probably have a minimal contributory value.

Excess site is *land or site area that is not necessary to support the use of the existing improvements situated on the subject property*. However, it may have its own highest and best use for expansion of the current improvement or for sale for another use.

For example, the owner of a house has an additional lot next to the house which he uses as a large side yard. The additional lot has its own unique legal description or could be legally divided from the site on which the house is situated, the site is likely considered excess. In such case, the contributory value is probably more in line with what the site could be sold for (minus any cost of subdividing, if applicable).

Now, let's look at how sites are identified and the analysis of other data so that all possible uses can be considered.

Identifying the Site

Before the appraiser begins to accumulate data for use in the site valuation, he needs to be sure that data is collected on the correct parcel of land. Sometimes the address is not enough, particularly when dealing with vacant land. Identifying the correct site involves obtaining and verifying the site's legal description. The test of a valid description of property is the ability to identify and distinguish that property from any and all other parcels of land. There are three basic types of legal descriptions used:

- Government survey system
- Lot and block system
- Metes and bounds system.

There are several important measures that must be remembered which relate to many legal descriptions.

Important measurements to know:

- Each **township** is six miles by six miles or 36 square miles.
- Each **township** is divided into 36 one-mile by one-mile township sections.
- Each **township section** contains 640 acres or six square miles.
- Each **acre** contains 43,560 square feet.
- Each **mile** is 5,280 feet.
- A **rod** or **pole** each consists of 16.5 feet or 5.5 yards.
- A **chain** consists of 66 feet, or four rods.

Government Survey System

The **government survey system** (also called **government rectangular survey** or **rectangular survey system;** some parts of the country also use the similar Virginia Military Survey System) is a *type of legal description for land referencing principal meridians and base lines designated throughout much of the country*. With the government survey system, a parcel of land is identified by directions and coordinates which count from these lines as reference points.

Additional north-south lines, called ranges or range lines, run parallel to principal meridians at six-mile intervals; and additional east-west lines, called township lines, run parallel to base lines at six-mile intervals. *This breaks up land into six mile by six mile squares* called **townships**.

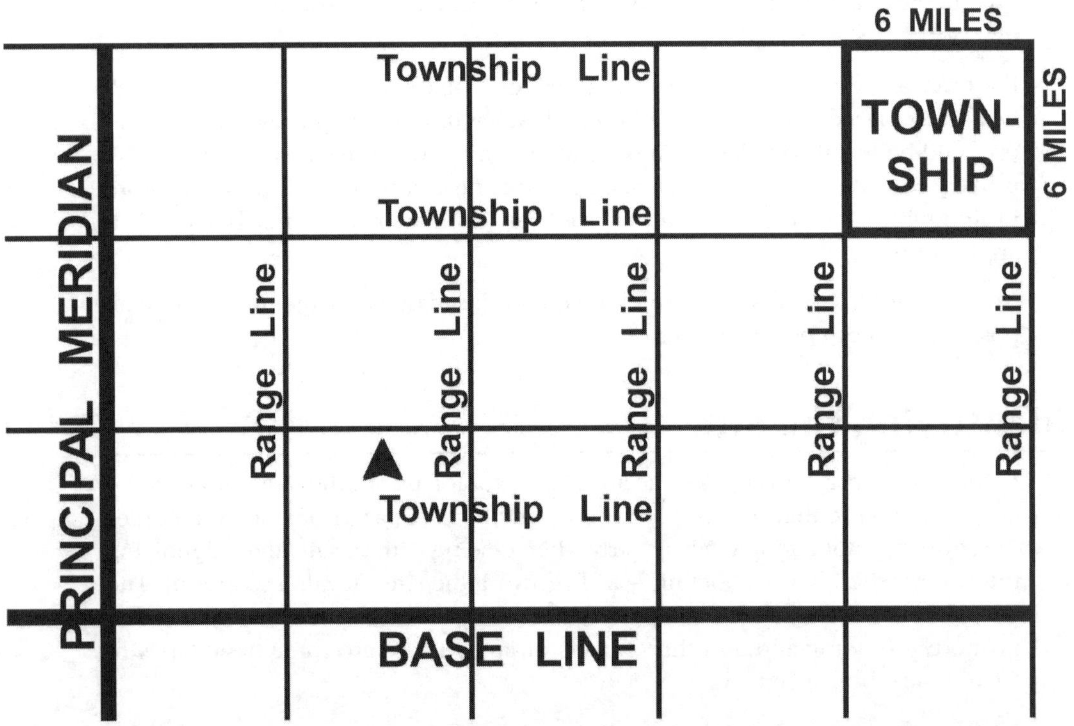

TOWNSHIP IDENTIFICATION: Using Principal Meridians and Base Lines (Each Principal Meridian and Base Line has a unique name or number.)

Sample township location.

The 36 square miles of a township are subdivided into 36 sections of one square mile (640 acres) each. Each section in a township is numbered sequentially, so that a person can locate her land by referring to the section number and subsequent references to half and quarter sections with compass points. Any portion of land that cannot be divided into equal fractional lots is designated as a **government lot**.

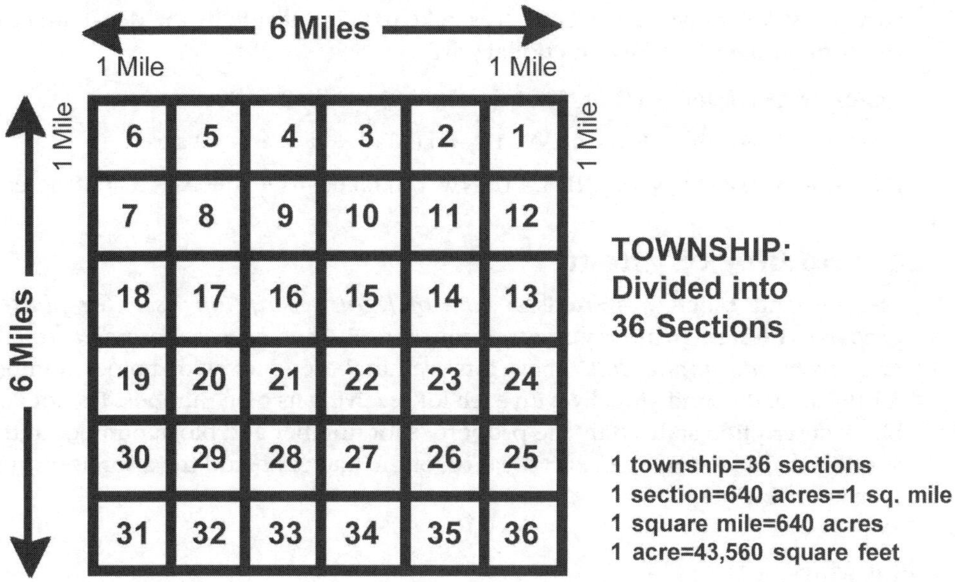

A typical parcel of land is located within a section. A legal description from this method would use directions and quadrants. Look at the following diagram.

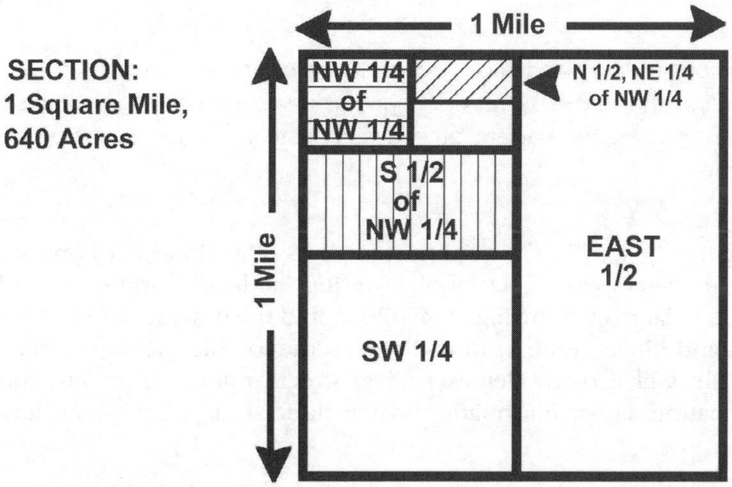

A legal description might read: N 1/2, NE 1/4 of NW 1/4. Always start from the end of the description and work backwards. We are talking about the NW 1/4, so look at the upper left corner of the section, then read the rest of the description to determine which part of the NW 1/4 is being talked about. Here are some examples.

Example 1: The S 1/2 of NW 1/4 is shaded like this: 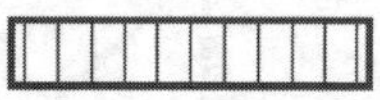

Example 2: The NW 1/4 of NW 1/4 is shaded like this: 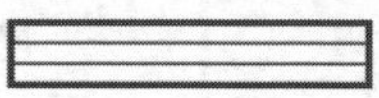

Example 3: The N 1/2, NE 1/4 of NW 1/4 is shaded like this: 

In addition to being able to locate a parcel of land within a section, for the appraisal exam, you may also need to know how to calculate the land acreage for a given parcel of land. With the government survey system, calculating acreage is rather easy. Again, start from the end of the legal description and work backwards from right to left. Since we know that an entire section of land in the government survey system always equals 640 acres, take 640 and divide by the denominators (bottom number) for each fractional part.

Example 1: For the S 1/2 of NW 1/4, take 640 ÷ 4 ÷ 2 = 80 acres.

Example 2: For the NE 1/4 of NW 1/4, take 640 ÷ 4 ÷ 4 = 40 acres.

Example 3: For the N 1/2, NE 1/4 of NW 1/4, take 640 ÷ 4 ÷ 4 ÷ 2 = 20 acres.

Lot and Block System

The **lot and block system** is *a type of legal description used for platted property*. **Platted property** is *any property that has been subdivided from a large tract into smaller lots.* These lots are numbered, first with a block number for the area, then individually with each lot receiving its own number. The lot and block description states only the property's lot number and block number in the subdivision, so to find the exact location of the parcel of land the appraiser must consult a **plat map.**

Plat Map

A **plat map** is *a detailed survey map of a subdivision (or other grouped lots of land), recorded in the county where the land is located.* Different jurisdictions have different rules about when land must be platted and a plat map recorded.

Example

In some jurisdictions, dividing land into five or more lots of less than five acres each may constitute that the land is being developed as a subdivision, which would require filing of a proposed plat map and other documentation with local authorities for special approval.

Plat maps are generally kept in the county recorder's office in a plat book, or available online in some areas. A plat book covering the land's location would contain the specific plat map, allowing someone to find the exact location of the lot using the lot and block number. In addition to the lot and block numbers, the plat map usually will also give details, such as streets, public easements, and ownership information. Other information may include zoning, elevations, and flood plains.

Example

In the following diagram, the legal description of the shaded area is Lot 19, Block 17 of Golden Valley Estate.

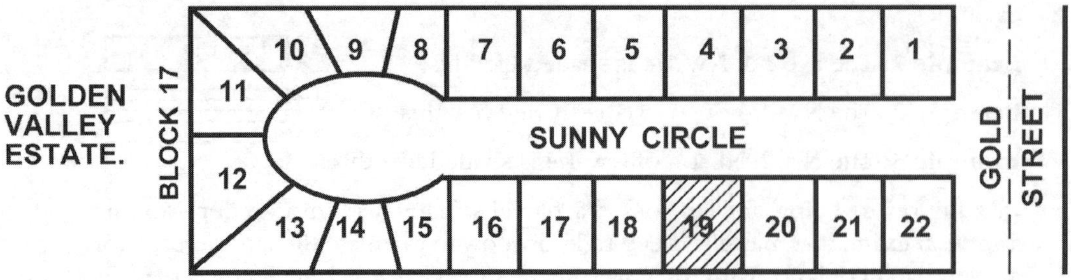

Sample Subdivision Plat Map: Golden Valley Estate, Block 17, Lots 1-22

Metes and Bounds System

The **metes and bounds system** is *a type of legal description that starts at an easily identifiable point of beginning (P.O.B.), then describes the property's boundaries in terms of courses (compass directions) and distances, ultimately returning to the point of beginning*. A legal description may also refer to monuments, which are fixed physical objects used as reference points.

Note: the point of beginning might also be referred to as the **point of origin**, and monuments are also called **markers**.

This type of legal description gets its name from the way land is described. From the P.O.B, a line is extended in a specified direction (metes). The line changes direction at specific points (bounds). The bounds are often permanent physical objects (e.g., monuments or markers). Care must be taken when selecting monuments to make sure that they are more or less permanent. A tree that is chosen as a monument may be cut down at a future date. A lake that is chosen as a marker may have the shore recede. Often the safest marker is a **pin**. A **pin** is *simply a rod that is driven into the ground.* This may be done by the original owner, a subsequent owner, or a surveyor.

The final important thing to remember about metes and bounds descriptions is that they must always return to the P.O.B. or the point of origin. Descriptions that do not return to the point of beginning are considered inadequate and inaccurate. They must be corrected if such an error exists, or if any markers or monuments have been moved or destroyed.

Example

A legal description of the land in the following diagram might read:

Beginning at a pin in the center of Miller Road, go SE 300 feet at an angle til the edge of the road meets another pin, then go due south 250 feet til you hit a pin at the adjoining property's fence, then go due west 350 feet to a pin at the edge of Miller's Pond, go due north 200 feet to another pin, then go due west 100 feet to a pin near the base of an old oak tree, then go due north til you hit the road, then NE at an angle to the point of beginning at the pin in the center of Miller Road.

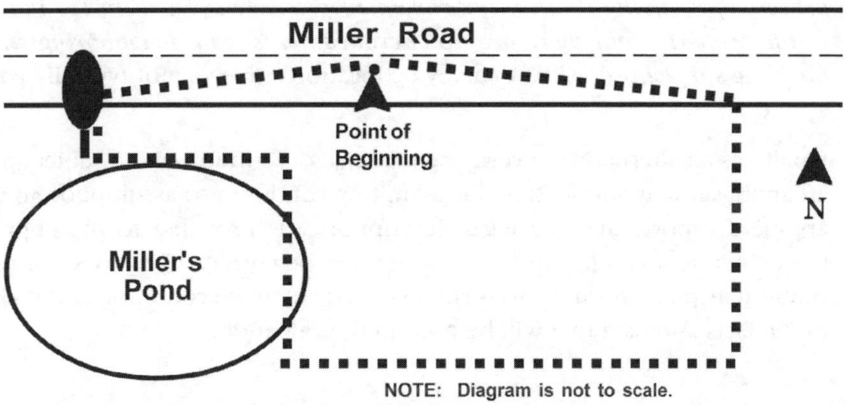

Sample Metes and Bounds Survey

Example

Calculating the area of triangular shaped parcels:

Regardless of which method has been used to describe a site, there may be some occasions when an appraiser must calculate the area of an irregularly shaped parcel, such as a triangle.

To find the area of an irregular shaped parcel, follow these steps:

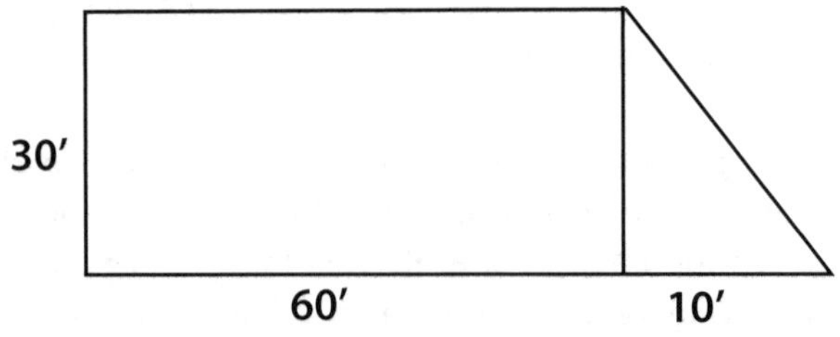

- Step #1: Calculate the area using Length × Width for the rectangular portion, and 1/2 × Width × Height for the triangular portion.
  - Rectangular area: 30′ × 60′ = 1,800 Square Feet
  - Triangular area: 1/2 × 10′ × 30′ = 150 Square Feet
- Step #2: Add both parts for the total area.
  - Total area: 1,800′ + 150′ = 1,950 Square Feet

Other Points About Site Identification

There are a few other things that appraisers should know about locating and identifying a site. First, although maps can be used to help locate property that has a government survey system or lot and block legal description, often no precise maps exist for property having a metes and bounds legal description.

Second, locating property by its legal description and verifying that it is the correct lot and more or less in the correct position is not the same as a survey. A **survey** is *the process of locating and measuring the boundaries of a property and identifying the improvements, encroachments, and easements that are associated with that land*. This process can be very expensive. A location survey is a less expensive alternative often used by lenders. A **location survey** is *the process of verifying that an improvement properly sits within the boundaries of the property, and there are no encroachments from neighboring structures onto the subject property*. A survey or location survey is not typically part of an appraisal.

Finally, as an alternative to verifying the legal description of the subject property, an appraiser may simply state (as a limiting condition or assumption in the final appraisal report) that the legal description was provided to the appraiser by the owner, lender, etc., and was assumed to be correct. This does not replace a physical inspection since this is still necessary to judge condition and verify some of the facts and data that will be used in the valuation.

Site Data Analysis

After the site has been identified, the appraiser can begin collecting and analyzing the appropriate data for site valuation. In addition to looking at general data on physical, economic, governmental, and social forces that are at work on a property, the appraiser will focus on the specific data factors that will affect the site analysis. Only after these factors have been considered can the appraiser decide which method to use for site valuation.

Specific Data Factors

There are many specific data factors that the appraiser will analyze with regard to a specific parcel of land. All data collected must be verified for relevancy, accuracy, and reliability. These specific data factors that are examined will fall into one of the categories that we already identified: Physical, economic, governmental, and social.

Physical Factors

Some would argue that physical factors are the most important data to be considered when examining the value of a site. In fact, the most important physical factor is size: Width, depth, shape, size of usable area, etc. The appraiser must be certain that the figures are correct. Configuration of the parcel of land is important as well (e.g., how the land sits in relation to the road, other parcels of land, etc.). A larger parcel is more valuable than a smaller one; a commercial parcel with more road frontage is more valuable than a landlocked one. Other physical factors specific to the property include the topography of the land (flat or hilly), drainage, soil type, and view. The presence or absence of utilities or other site improvements should be noted on the appraiser's site data form. The location of the lot within a neighborhood, position of the lot (e.g., corner, cul-de-sac,), and access to the lot are other factors that will be taken into consideration when determining value. For commercial properties, a corner lot is usually more valuable than an **inlot**, which is an *inside lot or middle lot*, but for residential lots the corner influence may or may not be beneficial. An analysis must be done to determine which type of lot is more valuable in a given residential market. This can be determined by examining and comparing information in the public records, as well as personally inspecting the site.

Economic Factors

Economic factors also come into play when examining the value of a site. Here relevant data concern the specific site, as well as the surrounding lots and the immediate area. The most important economic factor is the specific position or location of the lot with regard to market demand for that type of property. For example, is there need for more commercial development in the area, and can the site be used to fill that need? Is the property waterfront land? Do people in this area prefer corner lots and are they willing to pay more for them? Other economic considerations for the site may be relevant as well, depending on the unique circumstances in a given market area.

Other site factors include whether or not the current utilities are adequate for the land's ideal use, and what it would cost if it becomes necessary to upgrade them. Surrounding lot considerations include general conformity of lot size and use. Concerns in the immediate area would include positive and negative environmental factors that are present or likely in the near future. This data can be obtained from a number of sources, including personal inspection, public records, and general knowledge of market conditions and future plans for the area.

Governmental Factors

Governmental factors are also important considerations when examining the value of a site. The most important governmental factor is zoning. Most land would be worth more if used for commercial purposes instead of for residential homes, but the government limits the way a piece of property may be used. Governmental restrictions on land use also include public easements for roads or sewers, and building codes that restrict building size or placement. All of these factors can limit the buildable area of a site. Remember that some non-governmental restrictions can also impact value in the same way, namely deed restrictions and private easements. Other governmental factors that affect site value are taxes and public services. A heavy tax burden can lower the value of a site, whereas tax abatements can make a site more attractive. Public services that are close by, such as police and fire, can make a site more desirable than one where services are perceived as being too far away to provide adequate service and protection. All of this data can be obtained from public records.

Social Factors

Social factors may be a consideration when determining site value because of trends in the marketplace. Although, they are not as direct a factor as physical and government factors, the social dynamics and demographic trends in an area are still important. They can help determine what type of development might be best suited for the market. They are also useful in identifying area growth patterns, indicating which direction the area is growing. All of this data should be in the appraiser's general data files.

Highest and Best Use

After analyzing all aspects of the site, the appraiser is ready to determine the property's highest and best use. **Highest and best use** is *the most profitable, legally permitted, economically feasible, and physically possible use of a parcel of land*. Even if there are buildings or other improvements on the land, the appraiser still considers the site as if it were vacant and available for any use. This value is then compared with the value of the site as it is currently improved.

The higher value determines what is the highest and best use for the land.

This is one of the most important factors an appraiser considers before forming an opinion of value. The site may be more valuable if the buildings are torn down and the property put to a different use. The property owner would want to know these factors.

Determining Highest and Best Use

Determining the highest and best use for the subject property is an important exercise. The goal is to determine whether or not the property is being used for its most profitable permitted use. Highest and best use is always considered, although sometimes it is more important than others. Of course, with homes in the middle of a residential neighborhood, this is not an issue because the property is not likely to have a radical zoning change. But with commercial land or vacant land in an area that is changing, growing or expanding, this can be a significant point that needs to be addressed.

The appraiser must be aware of all governmental restrictions on a piece of land. Plus, the appraiser must also know the characteristics of that parcel of land. If the ground is too soft to support a large building, for example, this must be noted by the appraiser in determining the highest and best use for the site. Also, it is possible that a parcel of land would be more valuable if the current structure were torn down and replaced with a new type of building (e.g. an old house on land that is now zoned commercial). This type of situation should be noted in an appraisal report, along with all costs of demolition subtracted out from the final opinion of value.

Process For Determining Highest and Best Use

When determining highest and best use for a property, the appraiser gathers various values then compares these values. The steps can be summarized as follows:

- Estimate the value as if the land were vacant and available for any use.
- Estimate the value as the property is currently improved.
- Make a final determination of highest and best use by comparing the values arrived at in the first two steps.

Although in the end only two value estimates are compared, the process is really much more involved. These steps involve performing market studies, marketability studies, and other analyses depending on the potential uses considered. Remember, too, that all relevant costs must be considered as part of each value estimate. This may include repairing or tearing down the present structure.

One problem is that there are often numerous possibilities for developing vacant property, and the appraiser must at least consider all those that are possible. These possibilities should not be limited by the biases of the appraiser but should instead be based on the property and the market. The ultimate decision on highest and best use is reached by applying four tests.

Four Tests For Highest and Best Use

When evaluating ideal use, appraisers look at four tests for highest and best use:

1. Is the ideal use **legally permitted** on the property?

   Here the appraiser is primarily looking at governmental restrictions, as well as deed or other restrictions. Is the ideal use permitted with the existing zoning that is on the property? What is the chance of a zoning change? A zoning change must be shown to be reasonable or probable—not speculative.

2. Is it **physically possible** for the ideal structure to be built on the property?

   Here the appraiser is looking at the physical limitations of the site. Is the lot big enough to allow for the proposed structure with required setbacks, etc.? Does the topography of the site allow the ideal proposed structure? Will the ground support the weight of a large building?

3. Is the ideal use **economically feasible** on the property? (Note: This is sometimes referred to as financially feasible).

   Here the appraiser is looking to see if there is a market for the use being contemplated. Can the market support another use of this type in its supply and demand model? Are the other value principles conducive to this use?

4. Is the ideal use the **most profitable** for the property? (Note: This is sometime referred to as maximally productive).

   Here the appraiser is looking at net income that would be produced by the ideal use. Would other uses, building types, etc., produce a greater net income? Should other productive uses be considered which do not involve profit?

Although "most profitable" is the first point mentioned in our definition of highest and best use, it is actually the last consideration in the process. That is because all of the other steps are generally considered first before a determination of profitability can be made. If zoning laws do not permit a factory to be constructed on the property, then the appraiser should not waste time and resources performing a market study to see if such a usage is economically feasible. Once all the other points have been considered, then the appraiser can compare the possibilities to see what is indeed the most profitable use of the property.

There are other points about highest and best use which will be covered in more detail in other appraisal classes. From a site valuation standpoint, just understand that there is only one highest and best use for a property at any given point in time. Putting a site to its highest and best use results in maximum economic advantage to the owner. Determining the value of the site can be done using several different methods. This will be discussed in the next chapter.

SUMMARY

1. **Appraisal data** can be general data or specific data. **General data** cover the four great forces: Physical, economic, governmental, and social. These affect all properties in an area. General data focus is on local or national trends. General data resources are public records and filings, computer databases and the Internet, government offices, and professional publications.

2. **Specific data** can be subject property data (site and improvements), or comparative data about comparable sales and cost information. The data should be the most current and relevant available. Specific data resources include personal inspection, buyer, seller, broker, agent, contractor, property manager, county records, online, and MLS. Specific data must be researched for each appraisal.

3. **Market area** is a broad compilation of land uses and may contain more than one neighborhood or district. **Neighborhood** is a group of complimentary land uses. **Boundaries** can be natural or man-made, geographic, and type of property use—anything except those prohibited by fair housing laws. **District** is an area of one particular land use. Most properties in a neighborhood go through their life cycle together, which is growth, stability/equilibrium, decline, and revitalization.

4. Three methods used to identify site by legal description. **Government survey system** references principal meridians and base lines, and divides land into six by six square mile townships. A **township** has 36 sections (each one square mile), and a section has 640 acres (one acre = 43,560 square feet) and description has directions and fractional quadrants. **Lot and block system** uses platted property and a plat map shows lot and block numbers. **Metes and bounds system** starts at point of beginning (P.O.B.), uses compass directions and distances, may reference markers, and returns to the P.O.B.

5. **Data collection** is an important part of the appraisal process, as is verification and analysis. All data collected must be verified for relevancy, accuracy, and reliability. Timeliness must also be considered. Property specific factors that affect site value can be physical, economic, governmental, social—PEGS. Physical includes: Size, configuration, topography, drainage, soil type, view, utilities, location, and access. Economic includes: Location, utilities, conformity, and environmental factors. Governmental includes: Zoning, building codes, public easements, taxes, and services. Social includes: Social dynamics, demographic trends, and area growth patterns.

6. **Highest and best use** analysis of a site includes: 1. estimate land value as if vacant, 2. Estimate property value as is currently improved, and 3. Compare values to determine highest and best use. All potential site uses—and all costs of each use—must be considered. Four tests for highest and best use are: 1. Is the ideal use legally permitted on the property?, 2. Is it physically possible for the ideal structure to be built on the property?, 3. Is the ideal use economically feasible on the property?, and 4. Is the ideal use the most profitable for the property? Sometimes "maximally productive" is used instead of "most profitable" when a site use does not generate a profit (e.g., community center). There is only one highest and best use for a site at a given point in time. A site at its highest and best use gives the owner maximum economic advantage.

Chapter 2 Work Problems

1. If, through sales comparison, the value of similar parcels in the area is determined to be $32,000 per acre, what is the value of the parcel below?

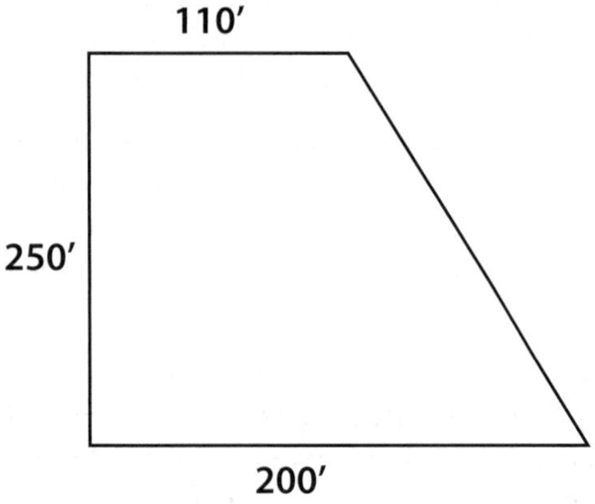

2. If property is selling for $500 per front foot, what is the value of frontage along one side of the SW 1/4 of a township section?

3. A property owner owns property described as "Section 7 of a Township." A public road runs along the east boundary. If he sells the N 1/2 of the NE 1/4 of the section, how much road frontage would the property owner still own?

4. A real property appraiser is examining the physical characteristics of a residential building lot that is 220′ by 110′. Per the jurisdiction's zoning code, a 30-foot set-back is required on all four sides. What is the largest two-story structure that could be placed on this lot?

5. A corner lot with commercial zoning currently is improved with a residential dwelling.
   - *Improved value—$150,000*
   - *As vacant—$200,000*
   - *Demolition cost—$25,000*

   Determine the appropriate highest and best use recommendation if demand for commercial sites is immediately recognized.

6. A metes and bounds description begins as follows:

   Beginning at a pin in the center of County Road 71, then following a line due south 180 feet to a pin, then due west 130 feet to a pin, then 40 feet due north to a pin, then due west 115 feet to a pin, then due north 140 feet to a pin in the center of the road.

   What is the distance indicated in the final call in an eastwardly direction to the POB, assuming a straight line?

QUIZ

1. ***If the subject's parcel has site area greater than is required for the existing improvements but does not have the usefulness required to consider it a sell-off parcel, what is this portion of the parcel called?***
   a. contiguous site
   b. excess site
   c. limited site
   d. surplus site

2. ***Which would be considered a general data resource?***
   a. economic forecasts for a particular market
   b. listing agent for a comparable sale
   c. recorded deed for the subject property
   d. seller of the subject property

3. ***A neighborhood can be defined by all of the following, EXCEPT***
   a. income level.
   b. natural boundaries.
   c. religious makeup.
   d. school district.

4. ***Which would be an area described as consisting of one particular land use?***
   a. district
   b. market area
   c. neighborhood
   d. region

5. ***Which means of site identification uses base lines and principal meridians?***
   a. government survey system
   b. lot and block system
   c. metes and bounds system
   d. Virginia Baseline System

6. ***Which means of site identification uses a point of beginning and monuments?***
   a. government survey system
   b. lot and block system
   c. metes and bounds system
   d. valley marker system

7. ***Which means of site identification uses recorded plat maps to locate a site?***
   a. county document system
   b. government survey system
   c. lot and block system
   d. metes and bound system

8. ***How many sections are in a township?***
   a. 6
   b. 16
   c. 36
   d. 640

9. ***How many square feet are in one acre?***
   a. 36
   b. 640
   c. 34,650
   d. 43,560

10. ***How many acres are in the following description? The S 1/2 of the SE 1/4 of the SW 1/4.***
    a. 20
    b. 40
    c. 60
    d. 80

11. ***You are appraising a corner lot in a residential neighborhood. What can you conclude about the value of the corner lot versus an inlot?***
    a. All lots have the same value regardless of position or size.
    b. Comparable sales must be analyzed to determine whether a corner lot is more or less valuable than an inlot in this particular market.
    c. The corner influence always makes a corner worth more.
    d. An inlot is always worth more in a residential neighborhood.

12. ***If a site is triangular in shape and has 100 feet of frontage and a depth of 150 feet, what is the site area in acreage?***
    a. .1537
    b. .1722
    c. .2222
    d. .2641

13. ***Which of the four tests for highest and best use considers zoning and other governmental restrictions?***

a. economically feasible
b. legally permitted
c. most profitable
d. physically possible

14. ***From a site valuation standpoint, how many different highest and best uses can a property have at a given point in time?***

a. as many as are legally permitted
b. at least two, but no more than four
c. every site is different so it is impossible to answer
d. only one results in maximum economic advantage

15. ***When might a residual physical segment of a land parcel be considered surplus site?***

a. if it is needed for future expansion of the subject's improvements
b. if it would be legally permissible to have another house built on it
c. when it cannot be legally sold separately from the subject or an adjoining
d. when it could freely transfer and be made available to the open market

16. ***Where are complimentary land uses typically found?***

a. district
b. neighborhood
c. restricted zone
d. subdivision

17. ***The time and distance relationship between properties and vital destinations, such as employment, shopping, recreational facilities, and major arteries is known as***

a. demographics.
b. efficiencies.
c. linkages.
d. situs.

18. ***A land parcel is 1/16 of a mile wide and 1/16 of a mile deep. If the parcel sells for $15,000 per acre, what is the total sale price?***

a. $3,750
b. $37,500
c. $375,000
d. $3,750,000

3

Chapter Overview

Once the appraiser gathers the appropriate data, the appraiser is ready to develop an opinion of value for the site. Several different methods are available, depending on the data available, the type of appraised property, and the scope of work in the assignment. First, this chapter will discuss the sales comparison method, which explains how to make adjustments to comparable sales to arrive at a value. Next, this chapter will review the allocation method, which details how to figure the ratios used and when to reassess them. Finally, there will be discussion about other ways to derive site value using extraction, land residual, ground rent capitalization, and subdivision analysis methods.

Key Terms

Allocation Method A site valuation method that separates the value of the land from the structures that sit on it by taking a ratio of the land or site value to the total property value based on a typical property in the area.

Comparables Other similar properties that have sold recently in a certain area. Also called **comps**.

Extraction Method A site valuation method that takes an estimated value of improvements and subtracts it from the total sales price to derive a figure for the land value.

Ground Rent Capitalization Method A method of valuing land based on the rent it generates in a given year divided by an appropriate capitalization rate.

Land Residual Method An income method of site valuation that attributes a certain part of the income produced by a property to the building or other improvement and then attributes the remaining income to the land.

Matched-Pair Analysis Process of determining the value of specific property characteristics or features by comparing pairs of similar properties. Also called **Paired-Data Analysis**.

Sales Comparison Approach An appraisal method that indicates the value of real property by comparing the property being appraised with other comparable properties. Data is collected and adjustments are made for differences. Also called **Market Approach** or **Sales Comparison Method**.

Subdivision Analysis Method A method of valuing land that could be developed, by taking the total projected market value of the finished project and subtracting all costs of development and entrepreneurial profit and incentive.

Using the Site Data

Determining site valuation is important for several reasons. Except in the case of raw land, the separate site valuation is rarely the end of the appraisal process. The site valuation figures derived from these calculations may be used for deciding highest and best use of the property, for adding a site value to the cost of building a structure or for isolating the site value to determine the insurance value of a building. But as with all steps in the appraisal process, the resulting opinion of value is only as accurate as the data collected. Attention to detail begins at data collection and continues through to the end of the appraisal.

Valuing the Site

Once all of the site data has been gathered, verified, and analyzed, the appraiser must choose a method of site valuation that will yield the most accurate results. After a method is chosen, the appraiser may need to gather additional data to implement the chosen valuation method. Different data is used depending on the method chosen. This additional data often include recent comparable sales information for similar properties in the area, as well as economic data for similar types of property.

There are several basic methods that the appraiser can use to perform a site valuation:

- Sales comparison method
- Allocation method
- Extraction method
- Land residual method
- Ground rent capitalization method

The first three methods use an analysis of comparable sales, and can be used for almost any type of property or site. The extraction method additionally employs costing methods. The last two methods use various income analysis methods to arrive at a value and can only be used for commercial or income properties. A sixth method, the **subdivision analysis method**, can also be used for some types of site valuations. The subdivision analysis method is typically used for large tracts of land that will be made into residential lots (although the method could be adapted for use when subdividing land into an office or industrial park). The following looks at each of these site valuation methods.

Sales Comparison Method

The **sales comparison method** is *a site valuation method that compares the subject land or site to other similar sites that have recently sold*. Adjustments are made to the sales for differences between those properties and the subject property, and the site value estimate is then based on this comparison to other sales. This is very similar to the sales comparison approach to appraising real estate, which is detailed in other appraisal courses and textbooks.

The first step for a sales comparison is to obtain data on other similar properties that sold recently in the same market area. These *similar properties* are referred to as **comparables** or **comps**. The comps should be as similar to the subject property as possible and preferably reflect the most current market conditions.

Next, market evidence is used to make adjustments to the price of the comps to account for differences between them and the subject. Finally, the resulting data is analyzed to arrive at an opinion of value for the subject property.

Comparables

Typically, several comparable sales, or comps, are used to arrive at a value figure. The comps should preferably be fairly recent sales, reasonably similar to the subject property, and part of an arm's length transaction. Comps where parties were related, sold as part of a liquidation sale (e.g., foreclosure), or had other unusual terms or concessions are typically eliminated. When an appraiser cannot verify or confirm the date of comps then the comps are unreliable and are often disqualified.

If there are not enough properties that have been sold recently in a given area, the appraiser may look in another similar area, or use comps with older sale dates, making price adjustments up or down depending on market conditions at the time of the sale. Any deviations that were used must be adequately explained in the appraisal report. The appraiser might also choose to use a different method of site valuation instead.

Adjustments

Adjusting properties is the process of making the chosen comps come as close as possible in features to the subject, so that meaningful price comparisons can be made. By this process, the sales comparison approach is able to approximate the value of the subject property based on objective data readily available in the marketplace.

The rule for adjusting properties is simple. The subject property is your base. Each comp is compared to the base. The subject never changes, so if a comp is missing something the subject has then you need to add something to make a positive adjustment to the comp to make them equal. If the comp has something extra the subject does not have then you need to take away from the comp to make a negative adjustment to it to make them equal. Here is a simple example.

Example

In a new home subdivision, 35 vacant lots have been sold and there are five left. Chris wants to buy a lot and is having it appraised. All of the lots sold in the past six months are the same size and shape. The only differences are the location of the lots and some of the lots are wooded.

For this example, assume corner lots are superior to inside lots (also called inlots) and wooded lots are superior to non-wooded lots. From comparing recent sales and using market evidence to arrive at adjustment figures, an appraiser can conclude the following:

	SUBJECT	SALE #1	SALE #2	SALE #3
Price	?	$14,000	$13,500	$14,250
Wooded	Yes	No +500	No +500	Yes
Location	Inlot	Corner lot-250	Inlot	Corner lot-250
FINAL	?	$14,250	$14,000	$14,000

The appraiser would likely conclude, based on the mode of the adjusted comparable sales data that a wooded inlot is worth about $14,000.

Remember that this is a simplified example. Although the appraiser tries to find comparable sales that are as close to the subject as possible, there are usually more adjustments than this—especially for houses or other improved properties. Also, the appraiser must do some additional calculations from gathered market evidence to determine the adjustment value for each feature that is different from the subject.

Determining Adjustments

A significant feature is *any difference that a typical buyer might pay more or less for and warrants an adjustment in the other comparable sales*. For example, if we analyze the data and determine that buyers will pay $10,000 more for a waterfront lot than one across the street, then this becomes a difference that we have to compensate for in our sales comparison. On the other hand, if buyers are paying the same price for a cul-de-sac lot as they are for a corner lot of the same size, then this difference would not warrant an adjustment. Typical items considered for adjustments are location of the lot, physical characteristics of the lot, and other things as dictated by the market. Other adjustments may be made for financing concessions or other unusual terms of sale.

Determing Adjustment Amount

Value adjustments for each feature that is missing or extra in a comp depend on a number of factors. The figures used can vary widely in different areas and may seem arbitrary, but an experienced appraiser can make a fairly accurate determination as to how much a particular feature affects the value of a property. Much of the basis for these figures is computed from a matched pair analysis of sales data for properties sold in the area.

Matched-pair analysis, also called **paired-data analysis,** is *the process of determining the value of specific property characteristics or features by comparing pairs of similar properties*. Ideally, there should only be one different characteristic between the pairs of properties being analyzed, so that feature can attribute directly to the difference in the sale price, or the contributory value of the feature.

Sequence of Adjustments

Discussion of the various types of adjustments give considerable weight to physical feature adjustments. In theory, these adjustments are less important than adjustments for date of sale, terms of sale, or financing concessions. In reality, appraisers effectively minimize these other differences by trying to select comps that are recent sales with conventional financing in the same neighborhood. This leaves the physical features of the comps as the primary differences that need adjustments. The **sequence of adjustments** in order of priority are: Property rights conveyed, financing concessions, terms of sale, date of sale, location of comp, and physical features or differences.

Allocation Method

The **allocation method** is *a method of site valuation whereby the value of the land is determined by establishing a typical ratio of site value to total property value in an area, then applying that same ratio to the subject property.* In other words, the allocation method recognizes that the utility of the site and the utility of the structure both contribute to the value of a property. Here is an example of the formula:

$$\frac{\textbf{Site Value}}{\textbf{Total Market Value of Property}} = \textbf{Allocation Ratio for Site}$$

Step 1: Identify Comparable Data

- Unimproved sites
- Improved sites

(The improved and unimproved sales should be located within the same market area, such as a subdivision.)

Step 2: Identify the Ratio of Site Value to Improved Value

- Divide the site value by the improved value

Step 3: Site Value Indication

- A range of value may be possible if several scenarios are examined

Example

An appraiser needs to establish a land value for a highest and best use analysis in an older, established neighborhood. However, the subject market has not had any vacant land sales for many years. The appraiser finds three other similar market areas, where there are both improved sales and unimproved sales. These market areas are as follows:

	Improved Sale	Unimproved Sale	Allocation Ratio
Sale #1	$200,000	$50,000	25%
Sale #2	$240,000	$60,000	25%
Sale #3	$250,000	$65,000	26%

Based on the mode of the data, the appraiser would probably conclude that 25%, 1:4 ratio, would be a reasonable allocation ratio to apply to the subject, which the appraiser has already concluded has an improved value of $225,000:

$225,000 × 25% (1:4) = $56,250

The indicated site value would be $56,250.

Points About Ratios

There are two important points for you to understand about the allocation method ratios. First, the appraiser would gather data on as many comparable sales as possible to establish an allocation ratio for any given area. A large number of calculations are needed to ensure the accuracy of the numbers.

Second, it is important to understand that these ratios can change over time. This depends on the desirability of the area, how fast it is growing, and the amount of vacant or undeveloped land that is available to satisfy market demand. The exact features or location of a lot are also a factor.

When the allocation method is used for residential land in newer subdivisions, or commercial properties in areas where there are lots of vacant land available for development, the ratios stay relatively consistent. However, the ratios still are subject to change over time. In fact, the National Association of Home Builders (NAHB) reports that site value represented about 11% of total property value just after World War II, while that number is around 35% today. If the site ratio goes higher than this, lenders become cautious when making a loan on a structure because a higher site ratio indicates that the primary loan value is for the land. Typically, the higher the site value the more superior the improvements. Analysis will help determine if a proposed improvement may not fit with the neighborhood. If not, a lack of conformity may be present, resulting in regression.

When the ratios are used for commercial properties in highly developed areas where there is little, if any, undeveloped land, the ratios must be recalculated more frequently. As the structure ages, the ratios will change. Deterioration causes an older building to be worth less than the land over time.

As an area continues to grow in desirability, the land becomes increasingly valuable for its inherent worth—regardless of what is currently on the land. The ratios will climb, and eventually the ratios get to a point where the land is more valuable than the structure that sits on it. This is common when residential land is rezoned for commercial purposes, but this can happen anytime new development comes to an area. If they really want the land in that particular location, people are often willing to tear down the present improvement.

This increase in site value ratio is less common for residential land, but it can happen in some situations. An example would be site values for unusually desirous lots in certain locations or with unusual features, such as waterfront lots, ravine lots, lots with a lake, lots with a specific view, etc. This can also happen in communities that are landlocked and have no more room to grow or annex additional land. If someone wants to live in the community, they may buy an older house and tear it down.

Note that if there are not enough comparable sales to establish an allocation ratio, sometimes it is acceptable to establish a ratio based on other data. For example, tax records and assessed values of properties can give an indicated ratio.

Extraction Method

The **extraction method** is *a method of site valuation that takes the depreciated cost of property improvements, and subtracts that cost from the total improved market value of the property to result in land value*. There are two situations where this method is extremely useful. The extraction method is most commonly used for new construction. By taking the total market value of a completed property and subtracting the cost of the improvement, the resulting amount is the site value.

Step 1: Calculate the Value of the Improvements

- Actual building costs, if being used in new construction
- Depreciated improvement value in existing properties
- Demolition costs, if highest and best use would be as vacant

Step 2: Site Value Indications

- Subtract the value of the improvements from the total improved property value

Example

The appraiser appraisers an 1,850-square-foot, single-family house for $165,000. Using the extraction method, she establishes the site value by subtracting the depreciated improvements from the improved value. Costing services indicate that the house will cost $77 per square foot to reproduce, and physical depreciation is estimated at 10%. The "as is" value of other site improvements is estimated at $5,000.

1,850 square feet × $77.00 per square feet	=	$142,450
Minus 10% depreciation	–	$14,245
Depreciated value		$128,205
Plus other improvements	+	$5,000
Total		$133,205

$165,000 – $133,205 = $31,795; the indicated site value would be $31,795.

Also, the extraction method is useful for existing properties when the value is primarily for the site and not the structures on it. For example, you could apply the extraction method to a piece of rural farmland. To figure the value of a large, 100-acre tract of land with a small farmhouse on it, take the total market value of the property and subtract the value of the house. Another example would be a property where the building has been condemned as uninhabitable. In this case, the structure is not contributing any value to the land but rather would incur a demolition cost, which would have to be subtracted from the market value to arrive at a true value for the land.

Land Residual Method

The **land residual method** is *a method of site valuation that attributes a certain part of the income produced by a property to the building or other improvement then attributes the remaining income (the residual) to the land.* By using an overall capitalization rate, the value of the land is then calculated. This method is useful when the value of the building or improvement is known and the value of the land is unknown.

The calculations for this method are not as complicated as they sound but are beyond the scope of this text. The complexity is determining how much income is contributed by, and thus attributed to, the land compared to the total property. Just remember that this is a variation of an income method, and primarily used for income producing commercial properties. Some of the income from the property is attributed to the improvement itself, and some income from the property is attributed to the land. This income figure is then capitalized at an appropriate rate to derive the value of the site separate from the improvements.

Step 1: Determine the Contribution of the Improvements

- Estimate the value of the improvements
- Allocate the net income attributable to the improvements

Step 2: Determine the Net Income Attributable to the Land

- Subtract the income to the improvements from total net income
- Residual net income will be attributable to the land

Step 3: Determine Land Value

- Apply direct capitalization of the net income to the land
- Use market derived capitalization rate
- Land value is then added to improvement value for total property value

Example

A warehouse facility is being valued. The appraiser is using the land residual method to verify another income approach. The building is valued at $600,000. Net income is $45,000 per year with 65% being attributable to the building. The market-derived capitalization rate for land is 8.75%.

$45,000 (total income to the property) × 65% = $29,250 (income to building)

$45,000 – $29,250 = $15,750 (income to land)

$15,750 ÷ 8.75% (0.0875) = $180,000

The indicated land value is $180,000.

The total value of the property is $600,000 + $180,000 = $780,000.

This method is mainly used as a verification of other income or appraisal methods. Also, the appraiser uses this method as a primary appraisal tool when there are few comparable sales in the area and the market income and capitalization rates can be identified.

Ground Rent Capitalization Method

The **ground rent capitalization method** is *a method of valuing land based on the income it generates in a given year and divided by an appropriate overall capitalization rate*. The appropriate overall capitalization rate is determined by examining other comparable sales and using the sale price and the annual net operating income that was generated in a year. Research must be done to obtain comparable sales of leased sites that are similar to the subject site. This is primarily a method used for commercial properties but could, in some cases, be used for residential properties built on leased land. Of course, the overall capitalization rate to be applied is usually derived after examining data from several comparable sales.

The calculations for this method are relatively simple. Take the annual net operating income of similar properties and divide that number by the site's sale price. That number results in the overall capitalization rate. Then take the annual net operating income of the subject site divided by that capitalization rate to derive a value for the subject site.

Step 1: Analyze Comparable Site or Land Sales

- Lease terms should be similar to the subject
- Net operating income should reflect a typical market
- Comparable sales should reflect arm's length transactions

Step 2: Calculate the Rate of Return (Capitalization Rate) of the Comparables

- Divide the net income by the sale price to find the capitalization rate (IVR)

Step 3: Apply the Capitalization Rate to the Subject's Net Income

- Multiply the net income by the rate to find the value (IRV)

Example

An appraiser is valuing a fast food restaurant site at a freeway interchange. The site is very similar in size to another site from which the appraiser recently gathered data. That site is located at the next interchange south with a slightly greater traffic count. It was valued at $800,000 and had a net income of $60,000 annually. The subject has a net income of $52,000 per year, which appears to be in line with the market.

Comparable:

$60,000 Net Income ÷ $800,000 = 0.075 or 7.5%

The market derived capitalization rate is 7.5%.

Subject:

$52,000 Net Income ÷ 7.5% (0.075) Rate = $693,333

The indicated site value is $693,333.

Subdivision Analysis Method

The **subdivision analysis method** is *a method of valuing raw land that could be developed, by taking the total projected sale value of all finished lots and subtracting out all costs of development*. The result is the value of the raw land.

The calculations for this can become quite complex. All direct and indirect costs of development must include many things: Construction of access roads, excavation, providing utilities to each lot, sales people to sell the lots, the interest the developer must pay to borrow the money, etc. Any cost the developer will incur before all the lots are sold counts as a development cost. In addition, entrepreneurial profit and/or entrepreneurial incentive must also be considered.

- **Entrepreneurial profit:** A figure derived from the market representing an amount received by the entrepreneur for his contributions and risk accepted in a project. Entrepreneurial profit is usually the difference between what the developed property could be sold for and the total costs of the project including land.
- **Entrepreneurial incentive:** This term could easily be confused with entrepreneurial profit, which is more closely related to actual profit, and

becomes somewhat complex in understanding the difference. But for a simple recognition of the term, this could be a dollar value attributable for the expertise and efforts provided in the connection of the development, such as the entrepreneur's expertise, skills, and involvement with development (e.g., leasing, selling) of the project. Entrepreneurial incentive can be thought of as the benefit that validates the efforts put forth in the project.

Example

A developer expects to get 50 lots from a land parcel and sell them for $30,000 each. If direct costs are $875,000, and indirect costs are $240,000, what is the land value if entrepreneurial profit is 10% of the gross sales?

50 × $30,000	=	$1,500,000
		$1,500,000
	–	875,000 (direct costs)
	–	240,000 (Indirect Costs)
	–	150,000 (10% entrepreneurial profit)
		$ 235,000 land value

When the developer considers the various costs, they must also take into account the length of the project, the cash flow during those months or years, and the time value of money. All of these calculations take into account not only interest paid on borrowed money but also the **opportunity cost** of having the money invested in this project instead of elsewhere. A complete example would take the total projected sales value of the finished lots and "discount" that to a present value, based on an acceptable rate for the money invested in the project. This number would be applied over the period of time that the project will take to develop, including the absorption time for the project to sell out. A financial calculator is a useful tool to accurately perform these calculations.

Chapter 3 Work Problems

1. A 10-acre residential tract is being valued. The deed restrictions limit one residence per tract, and no tract can be divided. Several other tracts, with varying acreage, have recently been sold within the same development with the same restrictions. Contributory value per acre of surplus land is $2,500. Some lots have lake access and some do not. Lake access lots sell for $10,000 more than those without lake access. What is the value of the subject?

	Subject	Sale #1		Sale #2		Sale #3	
Price	?		$62,500		$65,000		$70,000
Size	10 acres	8 acres		13 acres		11 acres	
Lake Access	Yes	Yes		No		Yes	
Adjusted Sale Price							

2. Using the mode of the indications from the allocation analysis below, what is the land value of a property if the improved value is $168,000?

	Improved Sale	Unimproved Sale	Allocation Ratio
Sale #1	$190,000	$57,000	
Sale #2	$150,000	$50,000	
Sale #3	$175,000	$52,500	

3. A rural property contains 193 acres of woodland and is improved with a 30-year-old ranch style house that has 1,458 square feet. The reproduction cost of the house is estimated to be $62 per square foot and depreciation is estimated at 40%. The "as is" estimated value of the other site improvements is $12,000. What is the land value if the improved value is $195,000?

4. An appraiser is valuing an office building. The building value is $375,000. Gross income is $30,000 per year. Vacancy and collection losses are estimated at 5%. Building expenses are $625 per month. The appraiser estimates that 72% of the income is to the building and that the observed capitalization rate is 10.25%. What is the value of the land?

5. A subject land parcel is producing an annual net income of $36,750. A very similar comparable has been located that recently sold for $435,000 with an annual net income of $41,650. What is the value of the subject land parcel?

6. A land parcel adjoining a lake is expected to yield 65 lots; 15 of which will be waterfront. The waterfront lots are expected to sell for $50,000 each with the remainder selling for $25,000 each. Direct costs are estimated at $920,000, indirect costs are estimated at 12% of the gross sales, and entrepreneurial profit is estimated at 8% of gross sales. What is the land value?

SUMMARY

1. **Sales comparison method of site valuation** compares the subject land or site to other similar sites that have recently sold. Adjustments are made to make those comparables or comps like the subject. The subject never changes. Adjustments are made for significant features using a matched pair analysis. Sequence of adjustments is financing concessions, terms of sale, date of sale, location of comp, physical features, or differences. Matched pair analysis determines value for specific property characteristics or features by comparing pairs of similar properties. When properties are similar, except for one feature, then the appraiser can attribute the difference in sale price to the contributory value of that feature.
2. **Allocation method of site valuation** is based on establishing a typical ratio of site value to total property value in an area and then applying that same ratio to the subject property. A similar formula can be used to derive a ratio for improvement value. An appraiser must look at as many comparable sales as possible to derive the ratio, and ratios can change over time. Factors that can cause ratios to change include change in property use, growth of an area, and deterioration of the structure. Sometimes ratios can be derived from other data, such as tax records.
3. **Extraction method of site valuation** takes an estimated value of improvements on the land, and subtracts that from the total value or sales price to derive a figure for the site value alone. The extraction method is commonly used for new construction. By taking the total market value of the completed property and subtracting the cost of the improvement, the resulting amount is the value of the site. The extraction method is also useful for existing properties when value is primarily for the site and not the structures on it.
4. **Land residual method of site valuation** attributes a certain portion of the income produced by a property to the buildings or other improvements and then attributes the remaining income to the land. This method uses a capitalization rate. It is used for commercial or investment properties.
5. **Ground rent capitalization method** takes the net operating income generated by property and divides it by an appropriate capitalization rate. This is primarily a method for commercial and investment properties. The calculation takes annual net operating income of similar properties and divides that by the sale price. This gives a capitalization rate, which is applied to the subject property's net operating income to indicate a value.
6. **Subdivision analysis method** takes the total projected sale value of all finished lots and subtracts all costs of development to arrive at a value for the raw land. All costs must be considered, including the time value of money. The future sales value is discounted to its present worth using an acceptable rate of return. This method is used for subdivisions, office parks, or other similar developments involving large tracts of land.

QUIZ

1. ***A comparable land sale has been identified for use in the valuation of a vacant residential building lot. The subject's view and topography are inferior. The subject's cul-de-sac location is superior. What is the indicated value for the subject site using market extracted adjustments?***

   Comparable sale price: $38,000
   View: $5000
   Topography: $2,000
   Location: $ 2,500

   a. $28,500
   b. $33,500
   c. $38,500
   d. $42,500

2. ***In a new subdivision, two homes that sold for the same price were identical, except that one was on a corner lot and one was an inlot. What can we conclude?***

   a. Corner lots are more valuable here because of the corner influence.
   b. The corner lot must have been smaller because corners always cost more.
   c. Inlots are more valuable, except in a distressed sale situation.
   d. In this market area, there is no price difference for lot position.

3. ***When hard and soft costs of development and the cost of the land are subtracted from the gross market value of a new subdivision, the remainder represents***

   a. entrepreneurial profit.
   b. observable depreciation.
   c. profit to builder.
   d. superadequacy.

4. ***If a vacant lot sold for $30,000 and a home sold for $120,000, the allocation ratio for land is***

   a. 1:3.
   b. 1:4.
   c. 1:12.
   d. 1:15.

5. ***An appraiser is using the depreciated cost of the improvements as a step in developing an opinion of the value for the land. Which land valuation method is the appraiser using?***

   a. allocation
   b. extraction
   c. land residual
   d. sales comparison

6. ***The subject is located in a newer but completely built-up neighborhood. The appraiser's scope of work includes developing a separate site value. Since there are no recent site sales in the subject neighborhood, the appraiser looks elsewhere to develop a site value. Across the street is a new subdivision where sites are selling for $25,000 and completed homes on similar sites are selling for $125,000. Improved, the subject is determined to be worth $175,000 via the sales comparison approach. Using the allocation method, what would the subject's site value be?***

   a. $20,000
   b. $25,000
   c. $30,000
   d. $35,000

7. ***A new structure will cost $850,000 when completed. Once completed, the structure will represent the highest and best use of the property. The improved property will generate NOI of $102,000. Capitalization rate for the building is 10.50%, and capitalization rate for the land is 6.25%. What is the indicated value of the land?***

   a. $90,000
   b. $145,000
   c. $193,000
   d. $204,000

8. ***To create a residential subdivision, which could generate $2,000,000 in sales for all sites once developed, a developer spends $375,000. Raw land value is***

   a. $375,000.
   b. $1,600,000.
   c. $1,625,000.
   d. $2,375,000.

4 Reasons for Separate Site Valuation

Chapter Overview

Separate site valuation is an important step in many appraisals even for properties that have structures on them. This chapter reviews some of the uses for separate site valuation—highest and best use, developing the cost approach, insurance value, economic life calculations, and property taxes—along with some formulas and examples. Next, the chapter discusses the role of the appraiser, noting Uniform Standards of Professional Appraisal Practice (USPAP) guidelines and obligations. Finally, some ways to increase the inherent value of land are explored through assemblage, plottage, and subdivision.

Key Terms

Assemblage The combining of two or more parcels of land into one larger parcel.

Economic Life The period of time, during the life of an improvement, over which the improvement contributes to the total property value.

Frontage The linear dimensions across the access (road) side of a parcel of land. (The first number of a lot dimension is the frontage.)

Insurance Value The amount that the property can be insured for, usually only representing the replacement costs of the structure and disregarding any value for the land.

Plottage Combining two or more parcels into one, with an increase in value over the value of the two parcels individually.

Remaining Economic Life The period of usefulness that a building has remaining as of the effective date of the appraisal.

Tear-down Properties When properties are worth less than the underlying land, and thus, people are willing to incur the costs of tearing down the present structure to use the land.

Uses For Separate Site Valuation

Appraisers need to conduct a separate site valuation to satisfy the scope of work in many appraisal assignments. Site valuation is an important analysis with many uses. The next few sections will explore several reasons why an appraiser might have to conduct a separate site valuation, even for property that is not vacant.

Determining Highest and Best Use

Highest and best use is the most profitable, legally permitted, economically feasible, and physically possible use of a parcel of land. This requires consideration of the site value, apart from any buildings or other improvements on the property. Highest and best use is always considered in every appraisal, but it is especially important for commercial land or land where zoning has changed. Sometimes the underlying land is more valuable than the structures on the land. (These are often referred to as **tear-down properties**.) If the property needs a separate valuation, an appraiser needs to advise the client if a change in property use is necessary to maximize value.

Using the Cost Approach

The cost approach relies on adding site value to the depreciated cost new of the improvements to indicate an opinion of value for the subject property. This determines if a project is economically feasible. For this reason, the appraiser must often have a means of determining a value for the site only. There are a number of ways to determine separate site value, as we discussed earlier in this textbook. In the next chapter, the cost approach will be discussed to help to understand the calculations. For now, consider the following formulas for a project that is economically feasible:

Total Market Value	**Depreciated Cost of Construction**
– Depreciated Cost of Construction	**+ Site Value**
---	-------------------------------------
Site Value	**Total Market Value**

Calculating Insurance Value

Insurance value is the amount that the property can be insured for, usually only representing the replacement costs of the structure and disregarding any value for the land. Since you cannot "lose" land, you only need to replace the building if it is destroyed. Thus, for insurance purposes, a separate site value is often required to determine the amount of coverage for which the insurance policy will be written.

Here is one formula used for insurance value:

Total Property Value
-- Site/Land Value

Insurance Value Amount

Remaining Economic Life Calculations

Useful life/economic life is *the time during which a building can be used for its intended purpose and generate more income than is paid out for operating expenses*. Keep in mind that although the value of land can go down because of external forces, the land itself is never said to suffer from physical depreciation. Site valuation comes into play because once a building's useful life (or economic life) is used up, then the property only has value as vacant land.

Even though the enhancements to land that make it a site could suffer physical deterioration, when appraisers talk about depreciation, they are talking about the structure on the land. Thus, a building's remaining economic life is the period of usefulness that a building has remaining as of the effective date of the appraisal. An appraiser arrives at the value of the building separately by taking the original cost of a building and subtracting out the portion of the building that is already been "used up", otherwise known as the depreciation. The value of the site is what is left over. So as the value of the building decreases from age, the proportionate value of the land/site increases.

Important USPAP Obligations

Land and site analysis can be broad and sometimes complex. There are many USPAP obligations that especially are important (but are not unique) to land and site valuation. In some cases, there could be numerous potential uses of a property, as well as extensive data that must be analyzed and interpreted. This likely would include identifying all restrictions on the site (e.g., easements, right-of-ways), as well as any rights that may be excluded in the ownership rights (e.g., mineral rights, water rights).

Possibly, there is an easement or visible encroachment on the property. Or, you may be inspecting a rural property and notice that there is or has been an old, abandoned and dilapidated automobile parked on the property. Such circumstance could lead to contamination when hazardous fluids from the automobile leak and absorb into the surface of the soil. Most certainly tanks, barrels, etc., which are used to store fluids provide for the similar hazard potential. In such case, an appraiser may need to consult with experts who specialize in such issues. The condition should certainly be disclosed and the affect on value should be analyzed.

Here are some key points excerpted from USPAP STANDARD 1 that are especially important as it deals with land and site valuation, whether improved or unimproved.

Note: The information is summarized for this discussion and is not, in all cases, a direct quote. Students are advised to refer to USPAP STANDARD 1 for the entire presentation.

Standards Rule 1-2(e) states (in part):

An appraiser must identify the characteristics of the property that are relevant to the type and definition of value and intended use of the appraisal including:

- Its location and physical, legal, and economic attributes
- The real property interest to be valued
- Any known easements, restrictions, encumbrances, leases, reservations, covenants, contracts, declarations, special assessments, ordinances, or other items of a similar nature
- Whether the subject property is a fractional interest, physical segment, or partial holding

The Comment to Standards Rule 1-2(i)-(v) states (in part):

The information used by an appraiser to identify the property characteristics must be from sources the appraiser reasonably believes are reliable.

Identification of the real property interest appraised can be based on a review of copies or summaries of title descriptions or other documents that set forth any known encumbrances.

An appraiser is not required to value the whole when the subject of the appraisal is a fractional interest, a physical segment, or a partial holding.

Standards Rule 1-3(a) states (in part):

When necessary for credible assignment results in developing a market value opinion, an appraiser must:

- Identify and analyze the effect on use and value of existing land use regulations...,
- Identify reasonably probable modifications of such land use regulations, economic supply and demand, the physical adaptability of the real estate, and market area trends; and develop an opinion of the highest and best use of the real estate.

Standards Rule 1-4(e) states (in part):

When analyzing the assemblage of the various estates or component parts of a property, an appraiser must analyze the effect on value, if any, of the assemblage. An appraiser must refrain from valuing the whole solely by adding together the individual values of the various estates or component parts.

A similar procedure must be followed when the value of the whole has been established and the appraiser seeks to value a part. The value of any such part must be tested by reference to appropriate data and supported by an appropriate analysis of such data.

Although the value of the whole may be equal to the sum of the separate estates or parts, it also may be greater than or less than the sum of such estates or parts. Therefore, the value of the whole must be tested by reference to appropriate data and supported by an appropriate analysis of such data.

Standards Rule 1-4(f) states:

When analyzing anticipated public or private improvements, located on or off the site, an appraiser must analyze the effect on value, if any, of such anticipated improvements to the extent they are reflected in market actions

Making Land More Valuable

While studying the motivation and methods for valuing a site, separate from any structures on it, remember that the land itself has some inherent value. The theories discussed about the value that land can be summarized as follows:

1. **Scarcity:** Land supply is limited and no more land can be created in any location.
2. **Indestructibility:** Land goes on forever; it always has potential to be utilized.
3. **Immobility:** Land cannot be moved and cannot be relocated from a bad location to a good location.

Other factors can come into play as well. Perhaps the most important is a corollary to immobility: Location. The location of land is the primary determinant of its value. The same amount of land is worth more in a downtown metropolitan city than it would be if it were located in the downtown of a small rural village. And the same amount of land is worth more as waterfront property than if it were not waterfront property.

Ways to Increase the Value of a Site

There are various methods to increase the value of land other than with improvements. Improvements to raw land to make it into a site can add some value to the land but the inherent value of the land is still the same. And if buildings are added, the value of the real estate is increased but not the inherent value of the land. The way to increase the value of land is to have more of it.

Assemblage and Plottage

Assemblage is *combining two or more parcels of land into one larger parcel.* This is typically done to increase the usefulness of the land. By allowing one larger building to be constructed on the larger parcel than could have been built on the smaller individual parcels, the value of the land has also increases. In fact, this one large parcel is likely worth more than the sum total of the smaller parcels. This is referred to as plottage. **Plottage** is *an increase in value (over the cost of acquiring the parcels) by successful assemblage usually due to a change in use.* By creating a larger parcel with more utility and higher and better use than the individual sites, the owner has successfully achieved an increase in the inherent value of the land and the individual land owners can benefit as well.

Example

Mega Company wants to build a new shopping center. They have picked out an ideal location where ten homes now sit. Those homes are worth about $100,000 each. Mega knows that the value of all 10 parcels together is $2,000,000. Instead of trying to buy each home for only $100,000, Mega is likely to offer the owners, $120,000 as an incentive for them to sell. If every home was purchased for $120,000, Mega's total cost would be $1,200,000—much less than the total value of the larger parcel. This will likely work at first but get harder near the end as the last few owners learn what is going on. These last few homes will likely cost Mega more money, but the owners have to be careful, too. If they are unrealistic about their worth to Mega's project or how high Mega is willing to go, they may get nothing. If these owners hold out too long for too much money, Mega may decide to design the project around them.

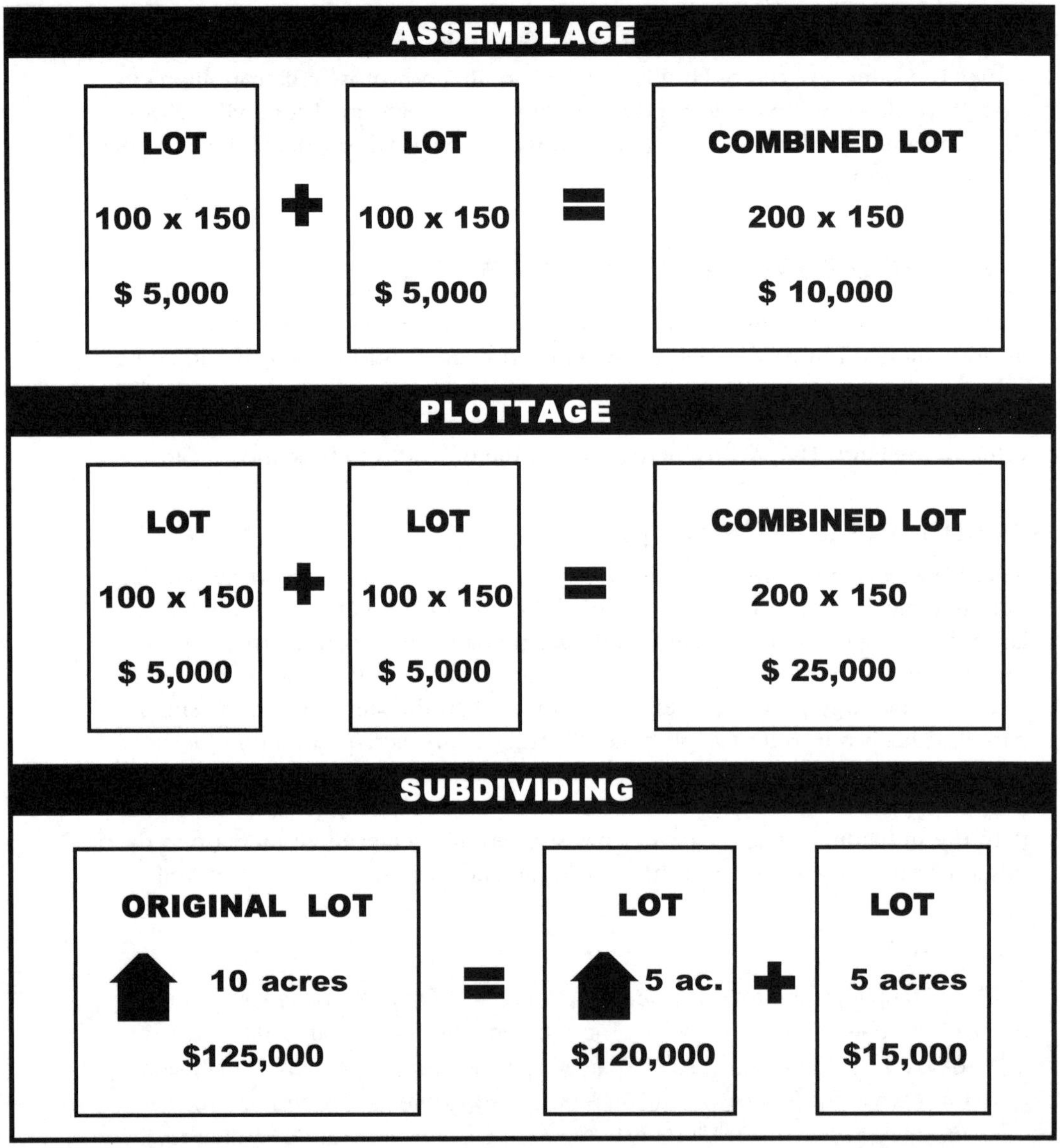

Assemblage, Plottage, Subdividing examples.

Subdividing

There are times when dividing property can increase value. There is not an official term for increasing value by subdividing land, but it amounts to "inverted plottage." Suppose you are appraising a house that sits on ten acres of land. If the property is not being used for farming or another specialized use that requires that much land, the appraiser might want to consider recommending to the client that the land be split into two parcels: One parcel of five acres with the house and another separate five-acre parcel. Of course the specific property and market would need to be analyzed, but it is very likely that the value of the house and five acres is not worth much less than the house and 10 acres. But now the owner has an additional parcel of land that can be sold or developed, thus increasing the total maximum productivity and profitability of the land. Zoning may even allow the land to be further subdivided into smaller lots, but many areas require platting and place additional restrictions on lots smaller than five acres.

Value of Frontage

As a corollary to assemblage and plottage, it is important to understand that the addition of some land is more valuable than other land. This is especially true for commercial property, which is compared by the front foot. Adding more frontage (dimension across the access side) makes land more valuable than adding more depth—even if the total amount of land added is the same. For example, if a lot is 100 feet by 100 feet, and a person buys up another lot that is the same size, the land is worth more if more frontage can be added (i.e., along the road) than if more depth is added. The lot still has the same total area, but a 200 feet by 100 feet lot is much more valuable than a 100 feet by 200 feet lot. (The first number in a lot size is front feet.)

Commercial properties value frontage more because it is more useful for business purposes. Adding depth still increases the value of the lot, but as the depth of a lot increases, the value per front foot increases at a decreasing rate. If a lot is 100 feet wide and 10,000 feet deep, how much would someone be willing to pay to make the lot 10,005 feet deep? Not much. The total value increase to the lot would be small.

Now suppose the lot is 100 feet wide and 10,000 feet deep, how much would someone be willing to pay for a few more feet of road frontage? More than that person would pay for more depth. Now remember, our examples are primarily for commercial properties. Generally, the marketplace does not make the same distinctions for residential properties. An increase in lot size (whether frontage or depth) generally contributes the same amount of extra value to a lot based on the total size of the lot. When comparing two lots that are not the same size, the marketplace ultimately determines how much additional lot area is sufficient to warrant an increase in value for the lot. A sales comparison of comparable properties in the market is the best way to determine if a larger lot is worth more, how much more the larger lot is worth, and what amount of additional land is needed to warrant an increase in value. The economies of scale theory implies that the larger the size of the parcel, the lesser the value per square foot. In other words, if the size of a 10,000 square foot lot is doubled to 20,000 square feet, the value will typically not double.

COMMERCIAL LOTS

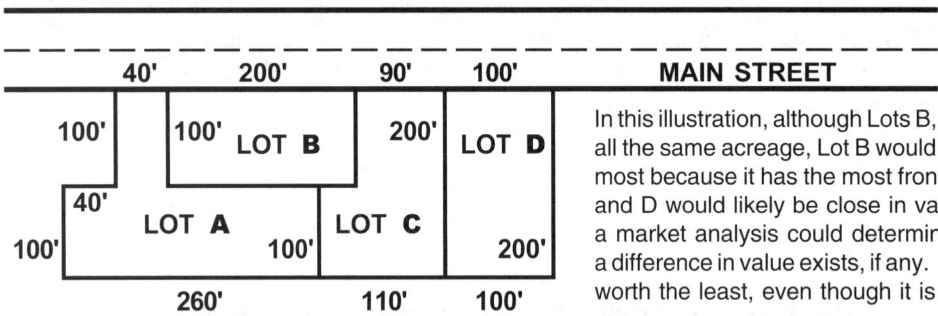

In this illustration, although Lots B, C, and D are all the same acreage, Lot B would be worth the most because it has the most frontage. Lots C and D would likely be close in value, but only a market analysis could determine how large a difference in value exists, if any. Lot A is likely worth the least, even though it is 50% larger.

RESIDENTIAL LOTS

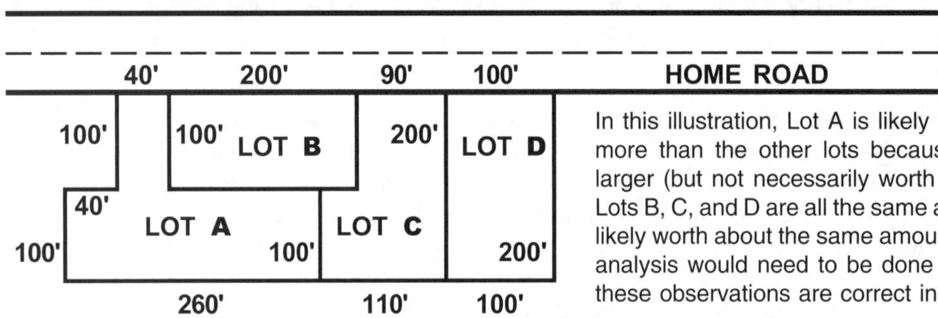

In this illustration, Lot A is likely worth a little more than the other lots because it is 50% larger (but not necessarily worth 50% more). Lots B, C, and D are all the same acreage, and likely worth about the same amount. A market analysis would need to be done to confirm if these observations are correct in this market.

Lot value examples.

SUMMARY

1. Appraisal assignments often require a separate site valuation. Many reasons include: Determining highest and best use, using cost approach, calculating insurance value, remaining economic life calculations, and figuring property tax.
2. Highest and best use requires consideration of site value separate from any structures on it, because underlying land may be more valuable if buildings are torn down (tear-down properties). Cost approach adds site value to construction costs to arrive at a market value (for a project that is economically feasible). Insurance value can be calculated by taking total property value and subtracting out site value (because land cannot lost or consumed).
3. **Useful life/economic life** is the time during which a building can be used for its intended purpose and generate more income than operating expenses. Land value can go down because of external forces, but the land never suffers depreciation. A building's remaining economic life is the period of usefulness a building has left on the effective date of the appraisal. As the value of the building decreases from age, proportionate value of the land/site increases. Once a building's useful life (or economic life) is used up, then property only has site value. Allocation uses a typical ratio of site value to total property value in an area, and then applies that ratio to the subject property. Ratios work because of the value theories for balance and utility.
4. USPAP has many requirements that, while not unique to land and site valuation, are very important in the development of an appraisal. An appraiser must identify the characteristics of the property that are relevant to the type and definition of value and intended use of the appraisal. This includes identifying all site restrictions (e.g., easements, ROW), and any rights excluded from the ownership (e.g., mineral rights, water rights).
5. Land is inherently valuable due to scarcity, immobility, and indestructibility. **Scarcity** is limited supply of land in a given area. **Immobility** is that land cannot be moved to satisfy demand. **Indestructibility** means land goes on forever and is not consumed nor does land wear out, but usefulness and value can change over time. Location is the most important factor in land value. 1. Land value is primary determinant of real property value. People buy land and its location first and the structure second. 2. Land derives value from market demand. There must be market demand for property in its location, or the land has no value.
6. Inherent value of land can be increased through assemblage or subdivision. **Assemblage** is combining two or more parcels of land into one larger parcel increasing usefulness of the site. If the larger parcel is worth more than the sum total of the smaller parcels, this is called **plottage**. Dividing a larger parcel of land can result in more utility and more value. Commercial land is when the frontage is usually more valuable than depth. (First number in a lot size is frontage.) For residential land, usually an appraiser compares total size of the land. In both cases, a market study must be done to determine any amount of value difference.

QUIZ

1. ***When the underlying land is more valuable after considering demolition costs than it is with the current improvements, what would the appraiser most likely recommend?***
   a. determine the present use is the property's highest and best use
   b. recalculate the site value until it is lower than the value of the structure
   c. recommend that the structure be torn down
   d. skip the highest and best use step in the appraisal

2. ***If the total market value of a property would be less than the construction cost of a newly built home, what does this mean?***
   a. the appraiser must have made a mistake in the calculations
   b. the home should be built, regardless of cost
   c. the project is not economically feasible
   d. the site value should be increased to compensate for this

3. ***A separate site value is sometimes necessary when determining an opinion of insurance value, so that the site value can be***
   a. added to the insurance value.
   b. added to the total market value of the property.
   c. subtracted from the improved value of the property.
   d. subtracted from the replacement cost.

4. ***When a building has reached the end of its useful life, then***
   a. the building must be completely renovated or torn down.
   b. the property is likely not at its highest and best use.
   c. the structure is worth more than the site.
   d. the site value is worth more than the value of the structure.

5. ***A client buys two adjacent parcels of land for $20,000 each. The appraisal shows that the combined larger parcel is now worth $40,000. What has occurred?***
   a. assemblage
   b. frontage
   c. plottage
   d. subdivision

6. ***A client buys two adjacent parcels of land for $20,000 each. The appraisal shows that the combined larger parcel is now worth $50,000. Which describes the resulting value increase?***
   a. assemblage
   b. frontage
   c. plottage
   d. subdivision

7. ***A client buys one large parcel of land for $200,000. The appraisal shows it could become 10 lots worth $25,000 each. This is an example of***
   a. assemblage.
   b. frontage.
   c. plottage.
   d. subdivision.

8. ***A fast food chain is looking for a new location. Assuming the cost of the lot is less of a concern than visibility of the business, which of the following lots would you recommend that the client choose?***
   a. 100 x 200
   b. 125 x 150
   c. 150 x 125
   d. 200 x 100

9. ***According to USPAP, information used by an appraiser to identify the properties relevant characteristics must be from***
   a. the client in the assignment.
   b. personal inspections of the property.
   c. public records on file in the jurisdiction.
   d. sources the appraiser reasonably deems to be reliable.

10. ***An appraiser must identify the characteristics of the property that are relevant to the type and definition of value and***
   a. the client's objectives.
   b. consistent with the current improvements.
   c. intended use of the appraisal.
   d. the value of the property.

5

The Cost Approach to Appraisal

Chapter Overview

This chapter introduces the cost approach to appraisal, defines it, and then explains when and why it is used. The differences between replacement cost and reproduction cost are explained with some points about when each is appropriate. The theory of substitution is discussed as it relates to the cost approach and the typical buyer. The theory of contribution is also explored along with an explanation of the laws of diminishing returns and increasing returns. Finally, this chapter discusses specific reasons and uses for the cost approach.

Key Terms

Cost The dollars needed to develop, produce, or build something.

Deficiency Property element that is less than necessary, interpreted by the market to be unacceptable, or an element that is functionally inadequate.

Depreciation A loss in value to property for any reason—physical deterioration, functional obsolescence, external obsolescence.

Overimprovement An improvement that exceeds the highest and best use for the site and does not increase the value of the real property in proportion to its cost.

Price The amount asked, offered, or paid for a property. *

Replacement Cost The estimated cost new of building the functional equivalent (substitute) of the original structure, using modern materials and workmanship and current day standards of size, layout, quality, and utility.

Superadequacy A feature of an improvement that is more than is necessary for the operation of the improvement.

Underimprovement When property improvements are not sufficient in relation to the highest and best use of the site. (i.e. acceptable balance of land and building value)

Value The amount of goods or services offered in the marketplace in exchange for something else.

**2010-2011 USPAP DEFINITIONS*

Defining the Cost Approach

The **cost approach** is *an appraisal method which estimates the value of real estate by figuring the cost new of replacing or reproducing the structure on the land minus depreciation and plus the value of the site*. Standards Rules 1–4 of USPAP states that when a cost approach is applicable, the appraiser must perform three distinct steps:

1. Develop an opinion of site value by an appropriate appraisal method;
2. Analyze such comparable cost data, as are available, to estimate the cost new of the improvements; and
3. Analyze such comparable cost data as are available to estimate the difference between cost new and the present worth of the improvements.

Step number one was thoroughly covered in the first half of this textbook where several different methods to value a site were discussed. Step number two has the appraiser calculate the cost new of building a structure on the site. Calculating costs will be covered in depth in Chapter 6. Step number three involves figuring the accrued depreciation of the structure and effectively discounting the new-build price to reflect its current condition. Depreciation is the loss in value to property for any reason. Chapter 7 will discuss several ways of figuring depreciation.

The newer the building, then the more reliable the cost method is in estimating value. Although the cost approach is most useful as an appraisal method for newer buildings, it can also be used when a replacement cost for an existing building is desired or for unusual buildings with few comparable sales (e.g., house of worship, school buildings, industrial plants, etc.). The cost approach is also useful to check the value derived from the other appraisal approaches.

Replacement vs. Reproduction

Before a specific cost method is chosen, the appraiser must know whether the cost estimate is for replacing or reproducing the improvements.

- **Replacement** (similar): The estimated cost new of building the functional equivalent (substitute) of the original structure using modern materials and workmanship and current-day standards of size, layout, quality, and utility.
- **Reproduction** (duplicate): The estimated cost new of replicating the original building, using identical materials, workmanship, construction standards, size, layout, quality, and utility present in the current structure (including any functional obsolescence, deficiencies, and superadequacies).

The type and definition of value, intended for use of the appraisal, along with the characteristics of the property, will decide whether replacement or reproduction cost will be used in a particular assignment

Usually cost estimates are done for replacing a building with one that is of similar size and utility. Most of the time, the cost approach uses replacement cost because a building that is built to today's standards is a preferred and often less expensive alternative. A standard insurance policy would normally only cover replacement costs for a building. Cost estimates for reproduction of a building are typically done for historical buildings, where it is important for a new structure to have the exact same look and feel as the original. Since this will cost more to re-build, a special insurance policy would be needed at a higher premium.

Cost Approach and Substitution

As we examine the cost approach, consider how it is connected to the theory of substitution. A typical buyer is one that is acting in his own best interests and would rationally and readily accept a less expensive alternative property. This is true because substitution implies that an informed buyer will not pay more for a home (or feature) than a comparable substitute. Assuming no delay, the typical, informed buyer would pick the less expensive substitute. Keep in mind that implicit in the definition of the word "substitute" is the fact that the structures are more or less comparable in quality, features, and utility.

Usually, a buyer of an existing home will not consider cost when making a purchase decision (although sellers often do). The buyer may look at the cost of other new buildings as a benchmark of value, or as an alternative, but not in deciding what price to offer. The buyer's perception of value and subsequent offer to purchase are dictated more by market conditions, comparable sales, or anticipated income, rather than the cost of a replacement home.

However, with new construction, comparisons are easier for the buyer because he can readily ask other builders the cost of erecting a similar structure. For example, builders cannot typically charge informed buyers different prices for the same home, unless some justification can be shown. The theory of substitution is also easier to observe with new construction, because there are more parcels of land available in a new subdivision than in established neighborhoods. This allows the typical buyer to readily choose from among various substitutes in order to maximize value while minimizing the price actually paid.

Substitution and the Typical Buyer

When examining the marketplace, the actions of a "typical buyer" are important because they present a way to predict what is most likely to happen. Unfortunately, buyers are not always informed and rational. This is especially true when dealing with residential property buyers who are looking for a home to occupy. Oftentimes they make a purchase decision emotionally, looking at the good side of a property they like and ignoring the bad. For example, depreciation is often overlooked in the buying decision because average buyers do not know how to quantify it and compare it between properties for substitution purposes.

Depreciation would not likely figure directly into a home buyer's decision making process, even though it is really in the buyer's best interest to do so. A home with better upkeep and more curb appeal will likely be more attractive to a buyer and sell more quickly, but this is rarely quantified by the buyer. The buyer may subconsciously know that an older home with more depreciation will have a shorter useful life, but she is unlikely to do any actual calculations to figure the costs involved with the depreciation, to ascertain the impact on value, and then rationally determine what to offer for the property.

The opposite is true for investors who likely will use depreciation figures extensively when deciding which property to buy. Furthermore, investors will examine the value of the subject property against the cost of erecting a new structure. In fact, the cost approach provides a theoretical upper limit of value in the marketplace in many cases. This is rooted in the theory of substitution. An informed buyer would not pay more for a property than the cost to build a comparable substitute.

In any case, the appraiser must fall back on the presumed actions of a typical buyer when trying to answer questions of value. It does not matter whether the buyer might be a completely rational investor or an unpredictable owner-occupant.

Cost Approach and Contribution

The cost approach is also connected to the theory of contribution. **Contribution** is *when a particular item (or feature) of a property is only worth what it actually contributes in value to that parcel of real estate*. This means that value is not equal to what something costs to build, but rather value is equal to what the market determines something is worth. This concept can be applied to a single feature in a building or to the entire structure. Overbuilding with features that the market does not want may lead to a structure that costs more to build than it is worth in the marketplace, and thus, the money that it cost to build cannot be recouped when the owner sells the property.

In other words, the contributory value of the feature or improvement is only equal to what the market determines a typical buyer is willing to pay for it rather than what it actually cost, but this contributory value can be positive or negative. A **deficiency** is *when a feature or component of a property is not adequate in the marketplace and results in a loss of market value (e.g., a small kitchen in a 4–5 bedroom home)*. A **superadequacy** is *when a feature or component of a property is too large, too expensive, or of too high a quality, such that its cost exceeds the contributory value of that item or feature (e.g., remodeling a kitchen at a cost of $25,000 when the property is only worth $100,000)*. The following discusses the law of diminishing returns and the law of increasing returns.

Law of Diminishing Returns

The **law of diminishing returns** says that *beyond a certain point the added value of another feature, addition, repair, etc. is less than the actual cost of that item*. (This may also be referred to as the law of decreasing returns.) In other words, you can add too much to a property such that you cannot increase the price enough to recoup the money that was invested. The owner may still want or need a feature in the property, but he should not automatically expect to get the full cost of the labor and materials back when he sells the property.

Law of Increasing Returns

The **law of increasing returns** says that *the added value of an additional feature, repair, etc. is more than the actual cost of that item*. This is referring to items that a property must have in order to compete in the marketplace, or features that are desired by the market. If the property adds these items, then the owner can recoup the cost when he sells the property. This is especially true if other competing properties in the market lack these items or features that the market desires. Of course beyond a certain point, the property can revert to the law of diminishing returns.

Example

A person is building a house and trying to decide how many bathrooms to put in it. The market currently dictates that a home must have at least one and a half baths. The cost of adding the half bath is relatively small, but a new house would be penalized in the market without it. This person is further deciding whether or not the master suite should also have a full bath. A market analysis by the appraiser shows that the cost of this additional bath can be recouped in a higher resale value when the new owner is ready to sell the property. But when an appraiser analyzes the market data for a home with three or three and a half bathrooms, then this forces the appraiser to conclude that the owners cannot recoup the cost of the additional bathroom in a future sale of the house. The house in the market would be worth the same with two and a half baths as it would be with three or more bathrooms.

Contribution and the Typical Buyer

Just as the actions of a typical buyer are important when considering substitution, those actions come into play with contribution as well. The value of an item or improvement is only equal to what the market determines a typical buyer is willing to pay for it and not what it actually cost. If you overbuild a house with too many features, then value would likely be less than the cost of building. This is referred to as an overimprovement. An **overimprovement** is *a property use where the cost of the structure exceeds the completed market value.* A property that is more expensive because it is too large or overbuilt with too many features will be shunned by a typical buyer who does not need that much space or those extra features.

Buyers do not care what a house costs to build as much as what other houses are selling for in the area. But a new building must have greater value than the cost to build it, or else there would be no new buildings without this profit motive. Still, the cost approach sets the theoretical upper limit on resale value.

An **underimprovement** is *when the property improvements are not sufficient in relation to the highest and best use of the site*. For example, a very small building on a large tract of land that could have accommodated much greater use - *the property does not achieve maximum value.* A typical buyer would be more willing to buy a property that is being used to its highest and best use, but a typical buyer will not overpay either. The market still determines what a typical buyer needs in that area, what the contributory value of those needs are, and what she would be willing to pay. That is why the cost approach to appraisal is used as a check against the sales comparison method and not in place of it. The cost approach can help determine value, but the market is the final arbiter of value.

Cost vs. Value vs. Price

The last section mentioned that cost does not always equal value. **Cost** is *the dollars needed to develop, produce, or build something*; **value** is *what a typical person would pay for something;* **price** is *what one person paid*. Market value is the most probable price that a property should bring in a competitive and open market. But the value of a parcel of real estate should not be confused with its price. **Market value** is *what a property is expected to sell for*; **market price** is what the property actually sold for. Both value and price may have nothing to do with what the property actually cost to build.

Why Use the Cost Approach?

The cost approach is a useful appraisal tool because it is the most objective of the three appraisal methods. With the cost approach, the appraiser simply counts items and multiplies the total number of an item by its cost, or the appraiser counts total square feet in a structure and multiplies that by a certain dollar amount. Once these figures have been calculated, there is some room for subjective evaluation of depreciation, but, overall, the cost approach is more objective than the other appraisal methods.

The cost approach cannot be used in all situations, (e.g., condominiums where fractional interests in land and community amenities cannot be readily determined) nor for all appraisals. Sometimes it is the primary valuation method, other times it provides support or confirmation for another valuation method. Even though the value derived from the cost approach may not equal market value, the next section will explore instances where the cost approach is an appropriate method of valuation to use.

Using the Cost Approach

There are many circumstances where the cost approach is an important valuation tool. Sometimes, it is the only method that can be used for valuing certain types of unique property. Other times, it provides additional information needed to evaluate a project or confirm another opinion of value. Here are different uses for cost approach.

New Construction

The cost approach is well-suited for valuing newly built structures. The newer the structure will provide for more recent, accurate, and relevant cost data figures. Furthermore, there is likely little or no depreciation to consider, which can pose a problem for valuing older properties with the cost approach.

Special Use Properties

The cost approach can be helpful when there is a lack of market activity as is often the case with single use, special purpose, or unique buildings (e.g., libraries and schools). There are usually not too many sales upon which to base a valuation using the sales comparison approach and no income data to use for the income approach.

Insurance Value

The cost approach is appropriate for calculating insurance value because insurance companies are usually interested in replacement costs for the structure. When this is the goal of the appraisal, site value is not part of the final opinion of value. (Reproduction costs can also be sought if desired by the insurance company or the client.)

Highest and Best Use

The cost approach can be applied to an evaluation of highest and best use for property. This is because the cost of building various proposed structures or renovating the one presently on the land is an important factor in determining highest and best use. Furthermore, the cost approach can be used to evaluate many types of projects and proposed developments to decide whether or not these projects should be undertaken.

Cost of Repairs

The appraiser can use the cost approach to determine the cost of repairing a structure, renovating it, or curing other deficiencies. This is an important assessment that must be considered in many appraisal assignments. The cost approach can provide the appropriate numbers to help make a recommendation to the client.

Support Other Valuation Methods

The cost approach can provide supporting evidence for other appraisal approaches to value. When performing the reconciliation process for an appraisal report, the cost approach can provide a means of checking or confirming the value conclusions reached using other methods. Remember, although the cost approach value does not necessarily equal market value, it tends to set the upper limit of value because of the theories of substitution and contribution.

SUMMARY

1. **Cost approach** estimates value of real estate by figuring the cost new of replacing or reproducing a structure on the land minus depreciation and plus site value. Cost approach is most accurate in valuing newer buildings. It can also be used for replacement cost of existing buildings (but depreciation can be difficult for old buildings) or special purpose buildings (if there are few comparable sales).
2. An appraiser decides if the estimate is for replacing or reproducing the structure. **Replacement** is building the equivalent of the original building using modern materials and reflecting modern functional utility. **Reproduction** is building an exact replica of a building. Reproduction is typical for historical buildings if a new structure needs the same look and feel as the original. Insurance usually covers replacement cost but covering reproduction cost requires a special policy with a higher premium.
3. **Substitution** says a typical, informed buyer would pick a less expensive substitute that is comparable in quality, features, and utility (assuming no delay). A typical buyer acts in his or her own best interests and would rationally accept a less expensive alternative. Buyers of existing homes usually do not consider cost approach when buying, but buyers of new construction can make cost comparisons by asking other builders the cost of a similar structure. Some owner-occupant buyers are not rational (i.e., do not consider depreciation). Investors compare numbers (e.g., existing structure vs. new construction).
4. **Contribution** says a particular item, or feature, of property is only worth what it contributes in value. Value does not equal cost; the market determines value. Contributory value of a feature/improvement is equal to what typical buyers in the market will pay for it—positive or negative. **Deficiency** is when a feature or component of a property is inadequate in the market (results in value loss). **Superadequacy** is when a feature or component of a property is too large, too expensive, or too high quality, so cost exceeds the item's contributory value. **Law of diminishing returns** is when beyond a certain point an added value of a feature, addition, or repair, etc. is less than the item's cost. **Law of increasing returns** is the added value of a feature, or repair, etc., and is more than the cost of that item.
5. **Cost** is the dollars needed to develop, produce, or build something; **value** is what a typical person would pay for something; **price** is what one person paid. **Market value** is the most probable price that a property should bring in a competitive and open market. The value of a parcel of real estate should not be confused with its price. **Market value** is what a property is expected to sell for; **market price** is what the property actually sold for. Both value and price may have nothing to do with what the property actually cost to build.

QUIZ

1. ***The appraiser does all of the following steps when performing the cost approach, EXCEPT***
   a. develop an opinion of site value.
   b. estimate the cost new of the improvements.
   c. estimate the difference between cost new and present worth.
   d. gather comparable sale data.

2. ***A loss in property value for any reason is called***
   a. deficiency.
   b. depreciation.
   c. law of diminishing returns.
   d. superadequacy.

3. ***If an appraiser had to value a historical museum, which of the following would most likely be used?***
   a. income approach
   b. replacement cost
   c. reproduction cost
   d. sales comparison approach

4. ***A buyer has decided to purchase a cheaper new build in a suburban subdivision instead of an existing home in the neighborhood. Which theory is at work here?***
   a. law of depreciation
   b. law of increasing returns
   c. theory of contribution
   d. theory of substitution

5. ***Instead of buying a house with a garage, a buyer purchases a comparable home that is $10,000 cheaper and then spends $5,000 to add a garage. Which theory is this?***
   a. law of adequacy
   b. law of detachment
   c. theory of contribution
   d. theory of substitution

6. ***A home owner has just added a third fireplace to his home in a neighborhood where most houses do not even have one. The third fireplace is likely a***
   a. deficiency.
   b. positive contributory value to the house.
   c. superadequacy.
   d. underimprovement.

7. ***When we refer to how much a property actually sold for, we are referring to***
   a. cost.
   b. market value.
   c. price.
   d. value.

8. ***Can the cost approach help with deficiencies?***
   a. No, the cost of a deficiency always has the potential to increase value.
   b. No, deficiencies are best left unidentified in an appraisal.
   c. Yes, it can help identify them and price the cost to cure them.
   d. Yes, it can help recommend an overimprovement to offset the deficiency.

9. ***Which cost is likely covered with a standard insurance policy?***
   a. cost to build an overimprovement
   b. cost to cure deficiencies
   c. replacement cost
   d. reproduction cost

10. ***Which is an element that would need to be addressed when using a reproduction cost that would NOT be addressed when using a replacement cost?***
    a. external obsolescence
    b. location of improvements
    c. physical deterioration
    d. superadequacies

6

Calculating Costs

Chapter Overview

The proper development of various costing components is important to the cost approach. This chapter begins by discussing hard costs, soft costs, and profit considerations for a structure. The chapter focuses on the square-foot method for calculating building costs, since it is one of the more common methods. This chapter includes detailed analysis and sample cost manual data to provide practice with a case study example. There are also brief discussions of other cost methods used in different situations: Comparative unit, quantity survey, unit-in-place, and index methods.

Key Terms

ANSI American National Standards Institute; responsible for GLA standards.

Comparative Unit Method A method for determining the cost of a building that uses the cost of recently built comparable buildings as a basis for estimating the cost of replacing the subject property.

Direct Costs Costs in a project that are not variable, such as labor and materials. Also called **Hard Costs**.

Entrepreneurial Incentive A dollar value attributable for the expertise and efforts provided in the connection of the development, such as the entrepreneur's expertise, skills, and involvement with development (e.g., leasing, selling) of the project.

Entrepreneurial Profit A figure derived from the market representing an amount received by the entrepreneur for his contributions and risk accepted in a project.

Gross Living Area (GLA) Residential space that is finished, livable, and above grade. Garages, finished basements, and storage areas usually do not count as GLA.

Index Method A method for determining the cost of a building by taking its original cost and multiplying that number by an index factor based on how long ago the building was constructed.

Indirect Costs Costs in a project that are variable (costs other than labor or materials). Also called **Soft Costs**.

(continued on page 71)

Building Costs

When using the cost approach, there are several different types of costs which must be calculated. Some of the more obvious costs for a new structure are building materials and labor, but there are numerous other costs involved with construction. Everything from taxes and insurance to zoning change fees and legal fees are all part of the costs to consider. Even the time value of money or the interest paid on the money used to finance the project must be considered for projects that will take a substantial amount of time to complete. The appraiser must be sure to consider all costs (direct costs and indirect costs) for a reliable indication of the cost new of a structure.

Direct Costs

Direct costs are *the costs in a project that are not variable, such as labor and materials.* These are also referred to as **hard costs**. In addition to paying for the labor and buying all the materials needed to build a structure, the contractor's has included their profit as part of the direct costs (since it is part of the construction contract). There are actually a number of different ways that the appraiser can calculate these direct costs when doing an appraisal.

Indirect Costs

Indirect costs are *the costs in a project that are, in many cases, variable—in other words, all costs for a project other than labor, materials, and equipment.* These are also referred to as **soft costs**. When looking at these costs, there are a number of items that the appraiser should overlook, such as taxes, insurance, sales commissions, professional fees for legal and accounting work, and many others. These fees are considered "variable" because they often increase as the project moves forward.

Direct Costs	Indirect Costs
Materials and labor	Real estate taxes during construction
Building permits	Engineering fees
Equipment costs	Architectural fees
Utility installation and cost	Appraisal fees
Contractor's profit	Accounting fees
Construction site security	Legal fees
	Insurance during construction
	Marketing costs and commissions
	Interest and expenses on any loans during construction

Entrepreneurial Profit and Incentive

Entrepreneurial profit and/or incentive is an amount of money left after all costs have been paid. This concept was introduced in Chapter 3. For many residential construction projects, the developers profit is stated as **entrepreneurial profit.** But, in some more complex projects there could be both. Here is a review of these terms:

- **Entrepreneurial profit:** Represents an economic reward received by the entrepreneur for his contributions and risk accepted in a project.

- **Entrepreneurial incentive:** Anticipated economic reward for the entrepreneur's or the developer's contributions of coordination and expertise of a project.

While this concept can be complex, when entrepreneurial profit and/or entrepreneurial incentive are specified along with the direct and indirect costs, it must be handled appropriately and included with the total cost of the project:

Direct Costs + Indirect Costs + Entrepreneurial Incentive and/or Entrepreneurial Profit = Total Cost

Entrepreneurial profit and entrepreneurial incentive may be presented as a dollar amount or as a percent of either the direct costs, indirect costs, or the total of direct or indirect costs.

Example

If direct costs of a proposed construction are $250,000 and indirect costs are estimated at $100,000, what is the total estimated cost of the proposed construction if entrepreneurial profit is 12% of direct and indirect costs?

$250,000 + $100,000 = $350,000

$350,000 × 0.12 (or 12%) = $42,000

$350,000 + $42,000 = $392,000

There are actually two types of profit that could be related to costing and care must be taken, so they do not become confused. The profit for the management company, general contractor, and other overseers of the project is included in direct costs. (This is listed as "contractor's profit" in the chart on page 70.) The reason this is included as a direct cost is because the amount is determined at the beginning of the project and as part of the contract for construction.

As seen in the previous example, entrepreneurial profit or incentive is a figure separate from the direct and indirect costs. With a new structure, this can be calculated by taking the final market value of the completed structure, minus the direct and indirect costs and the cost of the site. The difference is the entrepreneurial profit. This must be attractive enough so there is an economic incentive for the entrepreneur or investor to take on the project. If the project is not profitable then there is little reason for it to be pursued. As well, if market conditions change after the project begins and the value at completion is lower than expected or costs are higher than expected, then the entrepreneur risks loss on the project.

Value at Completion
\- **Direct and Indirect Costs of the Structure**
\- **Cost of the Site**

Entrepreneurial Profit/Incentive

Key Terms

Quantity Survey Method A cost approach appraisal method in which the appraiser counts the number and type of each part and material used to construct the building, adding costs for labor, profit, permits, etc.

Unit-In-Place Method A method for determining the cost of a building that estimates the cost of reproducing it by determining the unit cost of each of the component parts of the structure and adding them together based on actual need and usage.

Estimating Cost New

There are several different ways of determining the cost of building an improvement on a site. Cost sources used for most residential cost development typically reflect both direct and indirect costs. All of the methods discussed here can be used to estimate the cost of a new structure. When using the cost approach for an existing structure, however, some methods are more appropriate than others.

Before a specific cost method is chosen to price an existing structure, the appraiser must know whether the estimate is for replacing or reproducing the building. Remember: Replacement of a structure is building the equivalent of the original building using modern materials, workmanship, design, and functional utility; reproduction of a structure is building an exact replica of the original building. Reproduction cost also duplicates any negative aspects of the original structure.

Costing Services

Appraisers subscribe to costing services that provide estimated construction costs for numerous types of structures and other structural amenities. These services are offered in the form of an online service or as a published costing manual. These sources typically report costs for specific parts of a structure (useful for depreciation), as well as complete construction of various types of buildings. Some services publish books for different regions of the country, while other companies have multipliers to allow the cost figures to be adjusted for regional and/or local differences in material and labor costs.

Once the appraiser selects the appropriate method to use in the costing analysis, the subject improvements are matched with the costing service data for the most similar type of building, building features, and construction quality. This provides the appraiser an estimated cost in the appropriate unit (per square foot, construction component or element) for that area.

Although there are several resources for cost information, one of the most recognized is the Marshall & Swift costing service.

Some sample pages from Marshall & Swift appear on the next two pages. The facing page shows cost factors for a roof.

If the cost of a roof was being sought, then the individual cost factors for all of the relevant components for the style of roof would be added together. The cost per unit is then multiplied by the quantity needed (i.e., total square feet).

Assuming that a national cost source is being used, a regional multiplier would be used to bring the cost in line with local material and labor costs. This is commonly determined by the zip code of the project. On the facing page, you can see a sample page of local multipliers used by Marshall & Swift. The total is then multiplied by the multiplier to determine the cost new. Here is a simple example.

ROOFING

Notes

The unit of measure, "Square Foot of Roof Area," requires that the area of the roof, including consideration for roof slope and overhangs, be used. For buildings with sloping roofs, this area will be greater than the ground floor (i.e., footprint) of the building.

ROOFING – UNIT METHOD (ONLY)

To replace individual items, use the costs below:

Component		Quality Levels	
(Priced per Square Foot)	Economy	Standard	Custom
Roof Covers:			
Asphalt – Hot Mopped	$ .20	$ .25	$ .30
Built-up	1.45	1.65	1.85
Clay Tile	7.15	7.60	8.00
Concrete Tile	5.25	5.85	6.75
Copper	10.10	12.75	16.00
Elastomeric, Single-ply	5.30	6.85	8.90
Felt Paper	.11	.13	.15
Fiberglass	.85	1.10	1.55
Fiberglass – Corrugated	3.30	3.90	4.70
Metal	2.65	2.75	2.90
Plastic Tile	4.55	5.35	6.20
Roll Roofing – Composition	.60	.65	.75
Slate Tile	9.55	10.55	11.65
Shingles – Composition	1.05	1.20	1.35
Wood Shakes	2.50	2.85	3.25
Wood Shingles	2.40	2.90	3.30

Component (Priced per Linear Foot Unless Otherwise Shown)	
Miscellaneous:	
Coping	$ 12.90
Downspout	4.65
Fascia – Aluminum	3.40
Fascia – Board	2.60
Flashing	3.40
Gravel Stop	2.70
Gutter	4.65
Insulation – Batt (per square foot)	1.00
Insulation – Rigid (per square foot)	1.00
Sheathing (per square foot)	1.55
Soffit – Aluminum	3.10
Soffit – Board	2.60
Skylight (each)	250.00

Sample Cost Manual Page: Repair Cost Guide Factors for Roofing

Courtesy of Marshall & Swift—Reprinted from Marshall & Swift's *Home Repair & Remodel Cost Guide*—Used with permission.

LOCAL MULTIPLIERS

OHIO

	Baths & Kitchens	Ceiling & Wall Finishes	Doors & Windows	Elect., Plumb, & HVAC	Sitework & Ext. Walls	Floor Finishes	Roofing	Spec. & Equip.
430	.99	1.01	.98	.99	1.00	.99	1.00	1.00
431	.99	1.01	.98	.99	1.00	.99	1.00	1.00
432	.99	1.01	.98	.99	1.00	.99	1.00	1.00
433	.99	1.01	.98	.99	1.00	.99	1.00	1.00
434	1.07	1.08	1.04	1.10	1.06	1.04	1.05	1.07
435	1.07	1.08	1.04	1.10	1.06	1.04	1.05	1.07
436	1.07	1.08	1.04	1.10	1.06	1.04	1.05	1.07
437	1.01	.99	.99	1.05	1.00	.98	.99	1.00
438	1.01	.99	.99	1.05	1.00	.98	.99	1.00
439	1.03	1.00	.96	1.10	1.02	.98	1.09	1.05
440	1.09	1.15	1.07	1.09	1.09	1.08	1.10	1.12
441	1.09	1.15	1.07	1.09	1.09	1.08	1.10	1.12
442	1.09	1.15	1.07	1.09	1.09	1.08	1.10	1.12
443	1.09	1.15	1.07	1.09	1.09	1.08	1.10	1.12
444	1.04	1.05	.99	1.08	1.04	.97	1.07	1.06
445	1.04	1.05	.99	1.08	1.04	.97	1.07	1.06
446	.99	.99	.96	1.02	.99	.95	1.03	1.00
447	.99	.99	.96	1.02	.99	.95	1.03	1.00
448	1.00	1.02	.97	1.02	1.00	.97	1.00	1.00
449	1.00	1.02	.97	1.02	1.00	.97	1.00	1.00
450	1.03	1.04	1.03	1.02	1.02	1.00	1.04	1.02
451	1.03	1.04	1.03	1.02	1.02	1.00	1.04	1.02
452	.99	1.01	.97	1.02	.98	.96	1.04	1.02
453	1.01	1.02	1.00	1.04	.99	.98	1.03	1.01
454	1.01	1.02	1.00	1.04	.99	.98	1.03	1.01
455	1.01	1.02	1.00	1.04	.99	.98	1.03	1.01
456	1.03	1.04	1.03	1.02	1.02	1.00	1.04	1.02
457	1.00	.98	.98	1.03	.99	.97	.97	.99
458	1.00	.98	.99	1.03	.99	.97	.99	.99
OKLAHOMA								
730	.86	.85	.86	.87	.86	.90	.86	.83
731	.86	.85	.86	.87	.86	.90	.86	.83
734	.88	.85	.90	.88	.88	.94	.84	.84
735	.81	.78	.81	.81	.81	.84	.84	.77
736	.86	.84	.86	.86	.86	.90	.87	.83
737	.87	.85	.87	.87	.87	.90	.87	.84
738	.86	.84	.86	.86	.86	.90	.87	.83
739	.86	.84	.86	.86	.86	.90	.87	.83
740	.85	.83	.84	.88	.82	.83	.87	.80
741	.85	.83	.84	.88	.82	.85	.86	.82
743	.85	.83	.84	.88	.82	.83	.87	.80
744	.84	.82	.84	.88	.82	.82	.86	.81
745	.86	.84	.88	.87	.84	.87	.87	.82
746	.85	.83	.84	.88	.82	.83	.87	.80
747	.84	.79	.83	.88	.82	.85	.81	.79
748	.86	.84	.88	.87	.84	.87	.87	.82
749	.86	.84	.88	.87	.84	.87	.87	.82

Sample Cost Manual Page: Repair Cost Guide Multiplier Page

Example

The cost of a standard quality metal roof is being calculated with the total roof area of 625 square feet. The project also needs 25 feet of gutter and 10 feet of downspout. The building location is in the 44131 zip code.

25′ (roof size) × 25′ (metal [standard])	=	625′
625′ × $2.75	=	$1,718.75
25′ (gutter size) × $4.65 (gutter price)	=	$116.25
10′ (downspout size) × $3.40 (price)	=	$34.00
Sub-Total	=	$1,869.00
Local multiplier for roofing in the 44131 zip code	×	$1.10
Total	=	$2,055.90 (roof replacement)

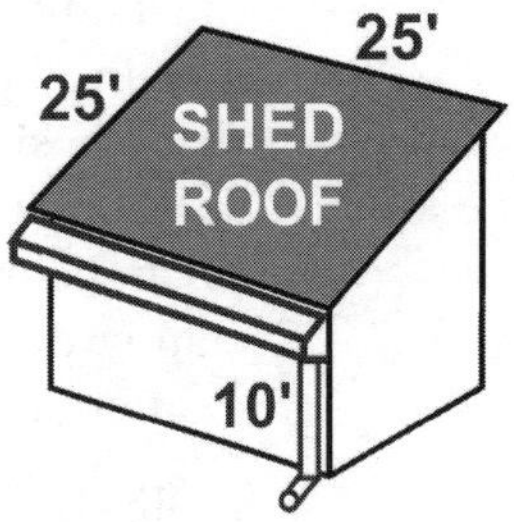

Calculating Area

When performing a cost analysis, it is important that dimensions are correctly calculated. Here is a review of how to calculate area, such as square footage.

Square footage is always calculated by using the outside dimensions of the structure. This is important because the building costs need to include the outside walls as well. The appraiser then follows national standards or locally accepted practices to determine which areas, if any, need to be subtracted from that square-footage total. For example, if an upper floor has a balcony, loft, or other open area to the floor below, then that open space would be subtracted from the upper-floor area. And, the appraiser must remember to multiply the area times the number of floors in the structure as appropriate for multi-story buildings.

For some properties, such as commercial buildings, the square-footage total may be divided by type of space usage. For example, the square footage may be divided between warehouse space and office space. In such a case, the different cost will be assigned to each type of space.

For residential property, non-living areas (e.g., garage space, screened-in porch, etc.) are subtracted from the outer dimension totals when figuring square footage. This is referred to as the gross living area. **Gross living area (GLA)** is *residential space that is finished, heated, and above grade.* In some warmer climate areas, GLA must also be cooled. Garages, finished basements, and storage areas do not usually count as part of the GLA, but finished attics can count if they have heat and electricity with finished walls and normal ceiling height. In some parts of the country, it might be customary to include substructure (below grade) space in the GLA. However, this is an exception only when a living area below grade is typical for the market and may be a very limited circumstance.

GLA and ANSI

Of course there may be accepted variations in your local market, but most commonly, national standards adopted by the **American National Standards**

Institute (ANSI) are observed for measuring the GLA of single-family, detached homes. Many recognized entities within the appraisal, real estate, and mortgage industry were active in creating what is referred to as American National Standard Z765-2003.

The standards are voluntary but widely accepted because they are constantly revised with input from many sources. When using these standards, appraisers must uniformly apply them. ANSI standards define "finished area" as "an enclosed area in a house suitable for year-round use, embodying walls, floors, and ceilings that are similar to the rest of the house." Garages and spaces below grade are specifically excluded. This is true even if the space is only partially below grade. Areas below grade are not included as finished floor area according to ANSI standards. The area is still part of the cost analysis but, of course, would require a different cost be applied.

DOING THE MATH. When calculating square footage, there are two formulas you need to remember: One for the area of a square or rectangle, and one for a triangle.

SQUARE or RECTANGLE—length times width

Area = Length × Width

$a = l \times w$

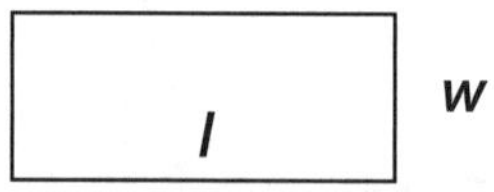

TRIANGLE—one half times base times height

Area = 1/2 × Base × Height

$a = 1/2 \times b \times h$

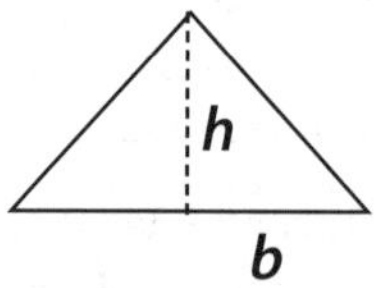

An appraiser can apply these formulas to each part of the structure until the entire square footage has been calculated. Figure the area of the individual parts of the structure (usually rectangles), then add them all together subtracting out the area of overhangs, garages, and other non-living spaces. Remember to double any part of the house designated as "two-story," and do not count finished basements or storage areas. Additionally, do not include a second level area that is open to the main level (e.g., a two-story foyer). (Note that all measurements must be in the same units before doing any calculations.)

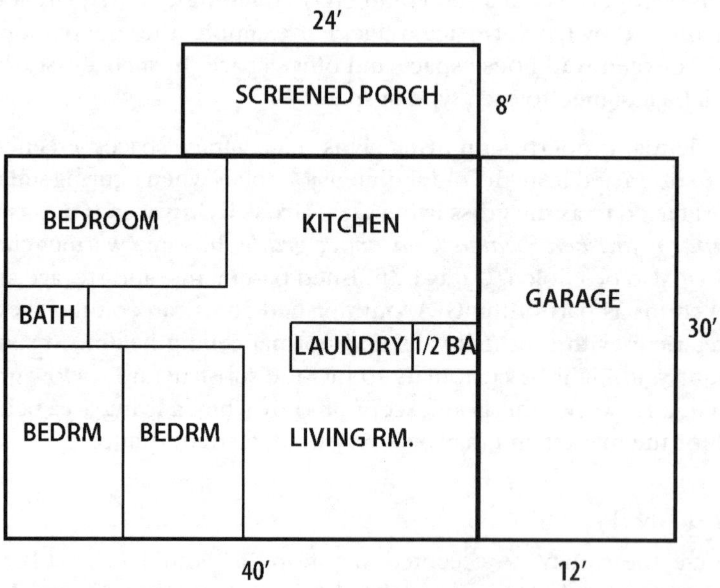

Costing Methods

Some methods of establishing cost are more appropriate than others, depending on the type and age of the property and whether the improvement already exists or is being proposed.

The appraiser's scope of work will set out the costing method appropriate to the appraisal assignment.

The cost approach methods are:

- Comparative unit
- Quantity survey
- Unit-in-place
- Index

Comparative Unit Method

The **comparative unit method** is *a common and relatively simple method for determining the cost of a structure based on known data*. Costs of similar structures are broken down into units of area. For residential dwellings, the unit is typically per square foot. There are several techniques the appraiser can use to develop a cost estimate using the comparative units.

1. An acceptable technique is to use the contract cost of similar buildings as a basis for estimating the cost of the subject property. Very often, the appraiser looks to prior appraisal assignments for new construction and uses the construction contract price, broken down per area unit (usually square foot) for that structure. That cost can then be applied to the subject's square foot area. If the comparable property from which the data was extracted is located in a different market, a location adjustment may be warranted. An appraiser must consider and apply adjustments when warranted for market conditions and any physical dissimilarity between the comparable property and the subject.

   Comparable New Construction Total Contract Cost

   $238,000 ÷ 2,250 Square Feet = $105.78 Per Square Foot

2. If construction contract data is unavailable and using a house as an example, a comparative unit technique is to use the total sales price of a newly constructed house that has sold. In order to use this technique, the comparable property's improvements must be at their highest and best use, supply and demand must be in balance, and the site value must be able to be determined. The appraiser would subtract the value of the site from the sale price to indicate a cost of the house. That cost would then be broken down into a unit, such as a square foot, and adjusted as necessary.

   Sale Price of Comparable Newly Constructed Home

   $287,500 – $35,000 Site Value =

   $252,500 ÷ 2,475 Square Feet =

   $102.02 Per Square Foot

For both of the above techniques, as was mentioned, unless the comparable data is similar, it is only used as a base or a benchmark—for significant physical differences, adjustments must still be made, which usually rely on costing services.

3. In most appraisals, when using the **comparative unit method**, the appraiser will rely on cost services for the base or benchmark cost. As mentioned earlier, the appraiser matches the subject property with the most similar type of building and building features that can be found from the costing service. The categories are broken down by style, type, quality, etc. This will give the appraiser an all-inclusive estimated cost per square foot to build that type of structure with those features in a particular part of the country. The appraiser then makes any necessary adjustments for variations in materials used or for other items or features not reflected in the base cost using the multipliers supplied by the costing service. This particular technique of the comparative unit method is sometimes referred to as the square-foot method.

Example

An appraiser is figuring the cost of a 1,250 square foot, one-story house in Chicago. Costing data for the Midwest region of the country, in which Chicago is located, shows total cost per square foot at $48.65. The cost per square foot can then be defined further by using a local multiplier for Chicago. If the multiplier for Chicago is 0.97, then the cost per square foot would be multiplied by the multiplier:

$48.65 × 0.97 = $47.19

1,250 × $47.19 = $58.987.50, the cost estimate.

Remember, this is just a simple example. A cost manual was used for the subject's region (Midwest). Cost manuals may also contain regional multipliers and other adjustment factors that must be included in the cost calculation for a building. Whether the appraiser uses different books or multipliers, they are designed to equalize regional differences in construction costs. Multipliers can also serve as a time adjustment based on when the manual was published or adjust for other differences.

Also, the example assumes the subject building is exactly like the one in the cost manual, so no adjustments were made. Appraisers must take into account differences between buildings described in the cost manual and the subject building. Materials used for the estimates are detailed specifically in the cost manual. Any differences must be accounted for by the appraiser. Other construction differences must also be accounted for, such as a warehouse with higher than normal ceilings might require using cubic feet as the unit instead of square feet (or some other adjustment factor). Accurate calculation of a subject's total area is an important skill.

Quantity Survey Method

Using the **quantity survey method,** *the appraiser counts the number of each type of part and material used to construct the subject building.* The total cost for all components is added together with an appropriate amount for the labor to put everything together: builder's profit, cost of permits, etc. This method could be used for anything, but might be commonly used to estimate the cost of reproducing a specialized building. However, most appraisers are not equipped or competent to the level needed to develop the method. In most cases, the services of a contractor or professional estimator would be required.

This method is the most detailed of the cost approaches, as it requires a thorough itemization of every building component used. This method duplicates the process a contractor goes through when determining a bid for a contract. All direct costs of building the structure are calculated—unit price of each material times the quantity needed, plus the cost of labor for assembly or installation. To get this figure, the appraiser adds all indirect costs—plans, permits, overhead, interest, taxes, profit, etc. An additional figure for the time value of money is often added to the profit figure, as well as a construction management cost and other costs for additional layers of management and profit—especially when an investor is involved, and the construction company or developer does not own the land.

Since the cost is figured so precisely, the appraiser must be able to make accurate estimates for labor and materials. Again, cost services can be useful.

Unit-In-Place Method

The **unit-in-place method** *estimates the cost of reproducing or replacing a building by determining the unit cost of each of the component parts of the structure, then multiplying the unit costs by the appropriate unit measure, and adding all of these unit costs together based on actual need and usage.* For example, rather than calculating the cost of each outlet and outlet cover as in the quantity survey method, the unit-in-place method considers the total number of outlets needed for the entire building and uses this to estimate the cost of the electrical service needed. This process is repeated for each main system or component of the building, often relying on cost services as the means of determining the cost figures.

Single-family Home—Sample Cost Breakdown

Component	% of Total	Cost
Pre-Construction		
Financing & Survey	.5	$919
Plans & Plan Checking	.5	919
Permits/Licenses	1	1,838
Structural		
Site Preparation	.5	919
Excavation	1	1,838
Foundation/Footings	4	7,352
Basement	6	11,028
Structural Framing	7.5	13,785
Interior Walls & Ceilings	3.5	6,433
Exterior Siding	3	5,514
Roofing & Flashing	5	9,190
Insulation	2	3,676
Fireplaces & Chimneys	2	3,676
Leaders & Gutters	1	1,838
Exterior/Interior Stairs	1	1,838
Doors, Windows, Shutters	2	3,676
Storm Windows, Doors, & Screens	1	1,838
Interior Finish Work		
Main Floor Covering	3	5,514
Kitchen Floor Covering	.5	919
Bathroom Floors	.5	919
General Hardware	.5	919
Kitchen Cabinets/Counters	3	5,514
Built-in Appliances	1.5	2,757
Shower Doors	.5	919
Bathroom Accessories	.5	919
Bathroom Cabinets/Counters	.5	919
Lighting Fixtures	1	1,838
Painting/Decorating	4	7,352
Utilities		
Water Supply	1	1,838
Waste Disposal	1	1,838
Heating & Cooling	4	7,352
Hot Water	1	1,838
Plumbing	4	7,352
Plumbing Fixtures	3	5,514
Electric Service	2	3,676
Electric Wiring/Outlets	2	3,676
Exterior Finish Work		
Porches/Patios	.5	919
Finish Grading	.5	919
Landscaping	1	1,838
Garage/Carport	5	9,190
Site Clean-Up	.5	919
Post Construction/Miscellaneous		
Interest, Taxes, & Insurance	1	1,838
Contractor's Overhead	4	7,352
Selling Expenses/Carrying Costs	5	9,190
Contractor's Profit	7.5	13,785
TOTAL COST	**100**	**$183,800**

Sample Construction Cost Manual Data: Residential Construction, Midwest

1-STORY HOUSE Living Area=1,200-1,499 sq. ft.

Economy Grade

Cost per square foot

Type of Work	Materials	Labor	Total
1. SITE WORK	0.10	0.80	0.90
2. FOUNDATION	3.00	4.10	7.10
3. FRAMING	4.35	3.25	7.60
4. ROOF	0.85	1.35	2.20
5. EXTERIOR WORK	3.75	4.50	8.25
6. MECHANICALS	2.60	1.90	4.50
7. INTERIOR FINISH WORK	4.75	4.85	9.60
8. KITCHEN/BATH	1.50	1.50	3.00
9. OTHER	1.00	1.50	2.50
10. OVERHEAD	1.50	1.50	3.00
TOTALS:	23.40	25.25	48.65

NOTE: Numbers are for example purposes only, and may not necessarily reflect current costs in your area.

Index Method

The index method estimates the cost of a building by taking its original cost and multiplying that number by an index factor based on how long ago the building was constructed. For example, a building built in 1990 cost $500,000 at the time of construction. A current index factor for that type of building might be 1.60. By multiplying $500,000 x 1.60, you get a present day estimated cost of $800,000 to build the same building. This method is actually not very common and is not considered by many as a reliable method of estimating cost—it is considered less accurate than the other methods, because it does not take many factors into account, and the original building cost must be known. But it can serve as a double-check against the other cost methods.

Chapter 6 Work Problems

Who am I?

Identify the costing method described below.

You cannot use me if you do not know my original cost. ____________________

I am ideal for new construction, as the standardized construction components have been identified. ____________________

I am the most complex and detailed. ____________________

I use cost data that is adjusted to the local market as a basis for estimating the cost. ____________________

SUMMARY

1. Cost approach has several types of costs. **Direct costs** (or hard costs) are not variable (e.g., labor, materials, equipment). **Contractor's profit** is a direct cost and part of the construction contract. **Indirect costs** (or soft costs) are variable—all costs other than labor and materials (e.g., taxes, insurance, fees). Indirect costs are often considered variable because they can change as the project moves forward. Profit for the developer and other risk-takers in a project is figured separately as entrepreneurial profit. **Entrepreneurial profit** is final market value minus hard and soft costs. Loss can result if market conditions change or costs go up.
2. Costs can be figured for **replacement** (similar) or **reproduction** (replica) of a building. The cost approach uses data from cost services or other sources that have information on cost of building materials and labor. Local multipliers adjust material and labor costs.
3. Living area is figured using outside walls times number of stories in a structure minus open spaces (e.g., lofts, balconies). Commercial buildings can be divided by type of space (e.g., part office, part warehouse). Residential property has non-living areas (e.g., garage, porch) subtracted from its size. **American National Standards Institute (ANSI)** says gross living area (GLA) is residential space that is finished, heated, and above grade. ANSI defines "finished area" as enclosed area in a home suitable for year-round use with walls, floors, and ceilings similar to the rest of the home. Garages and space below grade are excluded. Area is length times width for rectangles and squares.
4. The **comparative unit method** uses the cost, most often as a cost per square foot, of recently built comparable buildings as a basis for estimating the cost of the subject property. The information may be obtained through cost services or through local cost data. Key points of the comparative unit method include: Data from similar new construction projects, physical features can be adjusted between the subject and the comparable data as well as market conditions between the construction date of the comparable and the effective date of the subject appraisal report, and once adjusted, the comparable's construction cost is divided by its gross living area to find the per-square-foot cost, which is applied to the subject; directly related to market data
5. The **quantity survey method** specifies the number or quantity of each type of part or material used to build a structure. The total cost for these items is added together with the appropriate labor cost to complete the construction project; this includes permits, appropriate profit, etc. Key points of the quantity survey method include: Most accurate and detailed costing method, requires thorough itemization of every building material, labor and materials must be accurately calculated; inflation of labor and materials must be considered if proposed construction will span a lengthy time period; and not commonly used in appraisal on a regular basis.
6. The **unit-in-place method** estimates the cost of construction by calculating the unit cost of all component parts of a structure (e.g., framing, roof, HVAC, etc.) and adding these costs together. Key points of the comparative unit method include: Uses cost services for costing data, uses standardized components and specific cost data, and ideal for new construction because completion can be easily recognized
7. The **cost index method** (also called the **index method**) estimates the cost of a structure by taking its original cost and multiplying it by an index factor based on how long ago it was constructed. Key points of the cost index method include: Original building cost must be known, less accurate due to not considering numerous factors, used as a second check for other cost methods, and not common as a primary means of costing

QUIZ

1. ***All of the following are considered direct building costs, EXCEPT***
   a. contractor profit.
   b. labor.
   c. materials.
   d. sales commissions.

2. ***When hard and soft costs and the cost of the site are subtracted from the market value of a new building, the remainder represents***
   a. contractor's profit.
   b. entrepreneurial profit.
   c. observable depreciation.
   d. superadequacy.

3. ***A roof measuring 30 by 60 is being constructed at a cost of $8.00 per square foot. What is the price of the roof components in the localized market using a local multiplier of 1.10?***
   a. $480
   b. $720
   c. $14,400
   d. $15,840

4. ***Which of the following is most likely to be considered part of the gross living area?***
   a. attached garage
   b. finished basement
   c. finished and heated attic with normal ceiling height
   d. screened in porch

5. ***Which body is responsible for maintaining the voluntary GLA standards?***
   a. American National Standards Institute (ANSI)
   b. Appraisal Foundation
   c. U.S. Department of Housing and Urban Development (HUD)
   d. National Association of Realtors

6. ***Which walls are measured when calculating gross living area?***
   a. all exterior walls
   b. all exterior walls, plus finished basements
   c. all interior walls
   d. all interior walls, except finished basements

7. ***Which cost method uses data from the local market to develop the cost new of a structure?***
   a. comparative unit method
   b. index method
   c. quantity survey method
   d. unit-in-place method

8. ***Which is the most detailed and complex of the cost approach methods?***
   a. comparative unit method
   b. index method
   c. quantity survey method
   d. unit-in-place method

9. ***If the year a structure was built is known, which cost method could be developed if a factor were applied to the original building cost?***
   a. comparative unit method
   b. index method
   c. quantity survey method
   d. unit-in-place method

10. ***Which would be considered a direct cost associated with construction?***
    a. accounting fees
    b. insurance
    c. real estate taxes
    d. utility installation

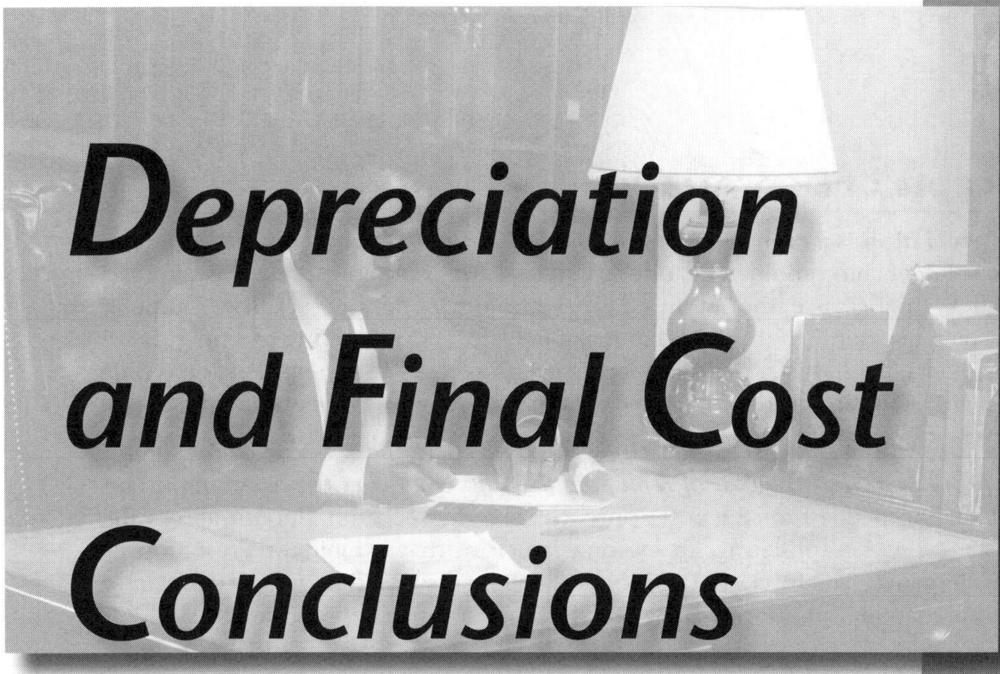

Depreciation and Final Cost Conclusions

7

Chapter Overview

After choosing the appropriate costing method to estimate the cost new of a structure or other improvement, the next step is to estimate an appropriate amount of depreciation to apply to the cost new. Estimating depreciation is considered to be one of the most sensitive elements of the cost approach. Credible assignment results require good support for the appraiser's depreciation estimates. Depreciation concepts and methodology will be thoroughly explored in this chapter.

Next, the steps in the cost approach leading to the final indication of value using costing techniques are discussed along with cost approach reporting and practical applications of the cost approach.

Key Terms

Accrued Depreciation The total accumulated depreciation.

Age-Life Depreciation A calculation that takes the effective age of a property and divides it by the total economic life.

Breakdown Method A method for calculating depreciation by taking a figure for each kind of depreciation and combining them into one number.

Curable Repairable Repairable or able to be fixed; something that can be fixed at a reasonable cost with the value added to the property being more than the cost of the repair.

Deferred Maintenance Physical deterioration created when required repairs are ignored.

Deficiency Property An element that is less than necessary, interpreted by the market to be unacceptable, or an element that is functionally inadequate.

Depreciation A loss in value to property for any reason—physical deterioration, functional obsolescence, or external obsolescence.

Economic Life The period of time, during the life of an improvement, over which the improvement contributes to the total property value.

Effective Age The age of a structure based on the actual wear and tear that the building shows from physical, functional, or external obsolescence, not necessarily the structure's age.

(conitnued on page 85)

Concepts of Depreciation

Depreciation is a *monetary loss in value of property for any reason*. Although the value of land can fluctuate due to external and economic forces that affect its highest and best use, the land itself is never said to suffer depreciation. Although the enhancements to the land that make it a site, and the improvements that we place on it, could suffer deterioration or obsolescence. Thus, depreciation is only applied to the structure on the land and other site improvements.

Accrued depreciation is the *difference between the current value of an improvement and the cost of replacing the improvement.* This is an important calculation needed for the cost approach. The depreciation amount allows the cost new to be applied to an existing structure that exhibits deterioration or obsolescence. The forces of depreciation will be discussed in greater detail later in this chapter, but, for now, the three forces that cause depreciation are:

- Physical deterioration
- Functional obsolescence
- External obsolescence

The first concept to understand is the important measurements to the life of a structure or other improvement—effective age, useful life, and economic life.

Effective Age, Useful Life, and Economic Life

The most common methods of depreciation revolve around certain measures of time in a structure or an improvement's life. As will be seen later in the chapter, when the discussion changes to depreciation calculations, the actual age of a structure or improvement is insignificant to depreciation. Rather, most common methods of depreciation examine the structure's effective age in reflection to the economic or useful life of the structure.

Effective Age

The **effective age** of a structure is based on all forces of deterioration and obsolescence (deterioration and obsolescence will be discussed later in this chapter). In other words, the effective age considers a structure's physical condition, how acceptably functional a structure is, and the external factors that influence a structure.

Using a house as an example, the moment the house is complete, the clock accounting for its actual age starts ticking and never stops. At the same time, the clock measuring effective age also begins. However, there are conditions or events that can make the effective age clock set back, or even jump ahead of the actual age clock.

Example

A house is 10 years old (its actual age). The owner replaces the floor coverings, repaints all of the rooms, spruces up the exterior, replaces dated lighting fixtures and otherwise brings the house to current day standards and tastes. Provided there are no other functional or external issues, the effective age clock will be set back—in this case to five years. Now the house has an effective age of five years and an actual age of 10 years. However, once the refurbishments become used and begin to age, the effective age clock ticks ahead as well.

Where did the five-year effective age come from in the previous example? Estimating the effective age of a structure or other improvement requires support by good judgment and reasoning skills on the part of the appraiser that comes through experience. The results of the cost approach can be skewed by not reasonably estimating effective age. Appraisers must be thoughtful and use great care as subjectively setting the effective age without support of sound reasoning and logic, as well as not communicating the reasoning and logic sufficiently in the appraisal report, are frequent causes for disciplinary action by state-appraiser regulators.

The next question to answer is: Could the estimated effective age be set back to zero? Theoretically, it could not. While a house may be significantly renovated or refurbished, even from the bare shell, there are likely certain elements that are not affected by renovations or refurbishment—the foundation, framing, etc. Therefore, those untouched elements are still subject to have some bearing on the estimated effective age.

Here are some other examples that could have a significant affect on effective age:

- A house that is neglected, abused, or has suffered damage due to a catastrophic event (e.g., earthquake, hurricane, tornado) could have an effective age greater than its actual age.
- A poor floor plan or a house built in an undesirable location could actually cause the effective age to be greater than the actual age.
- Left unaddressed, environmental issues such as radon, toxic mold, or site contamination could cause the effective age to be greater than the actual age.
- Changes in property uses external to a particular property (e.g., a factory or toxic waste dump) could cause the effective age of a house to accelerate, even though the house is functionally acceptable and maintained adequately.

Key Terms

External Obsolescence When something outside the control of a property makes it less desirable. External obsolescence can be locational or economic.

Functional Obsolescence When a building is less desirable because of something inherent in the design of the structure.

Incurable Something that cannot be fixed at a reasonable cost with the cost of the repair being more than the value added to a property.

Long-lived Item A component of the property that is not expected to be replaced during the life of a property.

Modified Age-Life Method A combination of the age-life method and the breakdown method of depreciation. This method can be employed when curable depreciation is attributable to obsolescence for which the depreciation can be readily recognized and calculated.

Overimprovement An improvement that exceeds the highest and best use for the site and does not increase the value of the real property in proportion to its cost.

Physical Deterioration Wear and tear on something due to age, the elements, or other forces.

Remaining Economic Life The period of usefulness that a building has remaining as of the effective date of the appraisal.

Short-lived Item A component of the property that is expected to be replaced during the life of a property.

Superadequacy A feature of an improvement that is more than is necessary for the operation of the improvement.

Underimprovement When property improvements are not sufficient in relation to the highest and best use of the site. (i.e. acceptable balance of land and building value)

Useful Life The period of time a structure or a component of the structure can be expected to function for the purpose it was designed for and relates only to physical deterioration.

These are just a few examples of how the effective age responds, and there certainly are numerous others. In some of these examples, some issues could be resolved, while other issues cannot be reasonably and practically resolved.

Useful Life and Economic Life

Useful life and **economic life** are also important concepts to understand and are best discussed together.

- **Economic life** is *the period of time, during the life of an improvement, over which the improvement contributes to the total property value, and is a reflection of all three of the forces of depreciation.* During this time, the improvement contributes positively to the property value. Economic life is a primary component of the age-life method and market-extraction method.
- **Useful life** *relates to the period of time a structure or a component of the structure can be expected to function for the purpose it was designed for and relates only to physical deterioration*. An example might be a component of the property, such as a furnace or roof that is expected to be replaced during the lifetime of a property. The concept of useful life is used in the breakdown method of estimating depreciation.

The terms economic life and useful life are often used interchangeably. If a distinction is made between these terms, economic life refers to the entire structure, and useful life refers to components of the structure. Estimation of the total economic life of a particular structure is derived from the market. The market extraction method of depreciation, illustrated later in this chapter, is one way that economic life can be mathematically calculated.

Remaining economic life references the period of usefulness a structure has remaining as of the effective date of the appraisal. In depreciation, an important measure is a building's remaining economic life, or the period of usefulness that a structure has left as of the effective date of the appraisal.

The effective age represents the number of years of the structure's life that has elapsed or has been used, and the remaining economic life is the number of year's life that is remaining of the structure. The total economic life of a structure is comprised by the total of the effective age and the remaining economic life.

Effective Age + Remaining Economic Life = Total Economic Life

As deterioration or obsolescence appears and continues, the effective age will become greater, and the remaining economic life will become shorter. Likewise, when a property owner refurbishes or renovates a structure, or other curable obsolescence is cured, the effective age will decrease and the remaining economic life will increase.

Again, an appraiser must not confuse or reflect the economic life to the actual age of a structure. There are many circumstances where the actual age of an older structure is far greater than its economic life.

Consider a 120-year-old house. This 120-year-old house could have a total economic life of 75 years, meaning that from its construction, if deterioration and obsolescence were not addressed, the house could have been used for its intended purpose, or generated more income than expenses for 75 years. However, the 120-year-old house has either received consistent maintenance and updating, or a major renovation, which has kept its effective age far below its actual age, and therefore, there continues to be some number of years of remaining economic life left.

So, adequately maintained, with acceptable functionality, and no external obsolescence is present, then the effective age of the 120-year-old house is 50 years. Given a 75 year economic life, the house has a remaining economic life of 25 years. If the same level of maintenance continues and no functional or external obsolescence becomes present, the effective age could continue to be 50 years and remaining economic life could continue to be 25 years.

50 Years Economic Life + 25 Years Remaining Economic Life =
75 Years Total Economic Life

Since many appraisals are performed for mortgage finance transactions, another important aspect of remaining economic life is its relationship to the amortization period of any mortgage that might be given with the property as collateral. Understandably, lenders want to ensure that the remaining economic life of a building is at least equal to the term of the mortgage. It makes little sense for the lender to make a 30-year mortgage on a building that is only expected to be usable for 15 more years. Furthermore, this illustrates why all mortgages contain clauses requiring maintenance and upkeep on the property. Deferred maintenance can rapidly devalue the collateral that backs the mortgage.

Physical Deterioration

Physical deterioration is *the actual wear and tear on something due to age, the elements, or other forces.* This type of depreciation is often observable during the appraiser's personal inspection of the subject property. Regular maintenance can slow this process; deferred maintenance results in items that need immediate attention. **Deferred maintenance** is *a physical deterioration that has occurred because of a failure to perform regular maintenance and upkeep.* Most deferred maintenance would be classified as curable (repairable) provided the severity of the condition is not beyond economical repair or replacement, but not all physical deterioration is curable.

Curable vs. Incurable

The test for deciding if physical deterioration is curable or incurable depends on the contributory value of the item that needs repair or replacement. *If the cost to repair or replace an item exceeds the value that that repair or replacement adds to the property value*, then the physical deterioration is said to be **incurable**. *If the item can be repaired or replaced at a reasonable cost and the contributory value added to the property is more than the cost of the repair,* then the physical deterioration is said to be **curable**.

This distinction is fairly clear with deferred maintenance items that are not operational or show advanced signs of neglect and need immediate attention (e.g., a broken furnace or widespread peeling paint). These items, if not repaired, would diminish the value of the property. Thus, deferred maintenance items are usually curable and should be fixed under normal circumstances. Oftentimes, the owner of a commercial or investment property will set up a replacement reserve fund so that money is available to address major expenses when they arise. Many owners of investment properties establish a **sinking fund**—*an account where money is deposited and allowed to accumulate with compound interest in order to cover a future expense.* If the item being inspected must be replaced, then the current cost of replacing the item with a new one is used as the depreciation figure. Generally speaking, if an item obviously must be replaced, it is considered deferred maintenance. For items that are in need of repair, though, the decision must be made whether to undertake the repair or replacement immediately or wait until a future date.

Short-lived vs. Long-lived Items

When considering different types of physical deterioration, the deteriorated elements are categorized further as short-lived or long-lived items. **Short-lived items** in a property are *those that are expected to be replaced during the lifetime of the structure*. This would include such things as carpet, an HVAC system, and paint. **Long-lived items** in a property are *those that are expected to last for the life of the structure*. This would include such things as the foundation and framing.

Short-Lived Items

For short-lived items, it may not be immediately apparent whether or not the repair should be made. For example, if a building has an older carpet that is beginning to show signs of wear, when should it be replaced? The amount of depreciation must be calculated before deciding whether or not it is worth the time, effort, and money to repair a property's shortcomings. After the calculation is made, then the depreciation figure must be considered along with the amount of value that the repair will add to the property. If the repair would add value to the property, the item would be considered curable (and likely classified as deferred maintenance). This type of repair should be done to maximize property value.

If the repair would not immediately add value to the property (as of the effective date of the appraisal), then the repair would likely be delayed until some point in the future. This repair would be classified as incurable, and an appropriate amount of depreciation would be subtracted from the value of the property.

Long-Lived

Long-lived items are almost always classified as incurable. Usually, these are not expected to need major repair or replacement during the building's useful life, and repairing them, if they can be repaired, is very expensive. Examples of incurable physical deterioration are wear or damage to basements, foundations, load-bearing walls, roof trusses, or floor joists. For long-lived physical deterioration items, the appraiser will typically use a percentage of the total value of the building to determine a depreciation value attributed to the incurable item.

Functional Obsolescence

Functional obsolescence is when *a building is less desirable because of something inherent in the design or nature of the structure*. This type of depreciation is observable during an inspection, but it may sometimes need to be confirmed with a demographics study or market analysis. For example, some older homes have two bedrooms in tandem—you must go through the first bedroom to get to the second one. While this feature can be observed, additional data is often needed to determine if this feature constitutes functional obsolescence. A demographics study may show that this feature is not a setback as long as the home has enough other, separate bedrooms to accommodate a typical family. A market analysis may show that this feature is a drawback when many newer homes are in the area, but not when the subject is in an area of older homes with the same feature.

Other examples of functional obsolescence are outdated home styles, out of date fixtures, or homes with only one bathroom. Unusual floor plans can also fall under the category of functional obsolescence. These undesirable features may be curable, because they can be fixed at a reasonable cost, like outdated fixtures, or these features may be incurable because they cannot be fixed without major cost or renovations, like a home's style. Remember, if the cost to repair/replace a deficiency is less than its contributory value, then it is curable; if the cost to repair/replace a deficiency is more than its contributory value, then it is incurable. The test for classification as curable or incurable is whether or not the cost of the renovation can be recovered when the property is sold. Major costs or renovations may be classified as curable if they would make a major contribution to the value of a home, such as adding a half bath.

Underimprovements and Overimprovements

With functional obsolescence, there are a few additional points that should be made clear. Functional obsolescence must be considered any time the improvements do not lend to the property's highest and best use. An **underimprovement** is *when property improvements are not sufficient in relation to the highest and best use of the site, thus the property does not achieve maximum value.* An **overimprovement** is a similar example of non-conformity where the improvements and, likewise the cost of the improvements, exceed the completed market value.

Example

If a 1,200 square foot house were constructed at a cost of $80,000 in a subdivision where the other homes all exceed 2,000 square foot and cost more than $150,000 to build, the 1,200 square foot house would be considered an underimprovement as it does not conform to the highest and best use of the site on which it was constructed.

Likewise, if a builder constructs a house at a size and/or cost exceeding other properties in a particular location, an overimprovement would result.

The analysis to determine if underimprovements and overimprovements are curable or incurable may become complex and often require the appraiser to consult with other professionals such as builders and architects.

Deficiencies and Superadequacies

A **deficiency** is when *a feature or component of a property is not adequate in the marketplace and results in a loss of market value.* A **superadequacy** is when *a feature or component of a property is too large, too expensive, or of too high a quality, such that its cost exceeds the contributory value of that item or feature.*

Whether a property feature is deficient or superadequate, it requires particular competency on the part of the appraiser in recognizing what market participants in a particular market expect and want. What might be considered deficient or superadequate in one market may not be in another. As well, what might be acceptable at one particular price point might be deficient or superadequate at another price point.

Example

> An appraiser may consider a three-car garage a superadequacy when attached to an 800-square-foot house. However, the three-car garage might be considered deficient when attached to a 12,000 square foot mansion in a market where four-car garages are expected.

On the other hand, the lack of a swimming pool in a warm climate market (at a particular price point) might be considered deficient, while a swimming pool in a cold climate market might be considered superadequate for which market participants will recognize little contributing value.

In many cases, cost estimates will be necessary to determine whether the deficiency or superadequacy is economically curable or incurable. There may be other circumstances where physical limitations could prevent the condition from being cured.

External Obsolescence

External obsolescence is when *something outside the boundaries of a property and the control of the property owner makes it less desirable*. The factors causing the obsolescence may be economic or locational factors.

Locational examples will vary depending on the nature of the property and the particular market but will hold true in most residential applications. Examples of locational external obsolescence include:

- Declining neighborhood
- Nearby landfill
- Noise and traffic from a highway
- Nearby railway
- Industrial exposure

Usually, economic considerations are an issue in non-residential applications and, again, are determined by the market. Examples of economic external obsolescence include:

- A structure or facility that can no longer be supported by the market economics and some overimprovements

Example

> The closing of a plant may cause economic external obsolescence, if the plant was important to an area's economic base. If there is little prospect of another use for the facility, it will create an economic external obsolescence.

External economic obsolescence may or may not be observable and often requires additional research. This additional research typically looks at the cause of the problem and the likelihood that it will continue, as well as research into the effect that the external obsolescence has on the market value of the property. In the previous example, the appraiser must consider whether the plant shutdown is permanent or temporary or if there are any parties interested in buying the facility.

External obsolescence is, in almost all instances, incurable—property owners can typically do little to stop or change these conditions. Even when action can be taken, such as trying to close a landfill, the outcome is uncertain and often far into the future. Such actions do not make something curable until the circumstance has actually changed. Thus, when the effective date of the appraisal is current, the condition is incurable.

Physical vs. Functional vs. External

It is sometimes confusing to sort out which cause of depreciation is at the root of the monetary loss. For example, if the outside of a house being appraised has been painted a very strong color that would meet with significant objection from the market, is the condition physical or functional? In this case, the loss in value due to the objectionable color is a functional obsolescence, as it is something inherent in the design or nature of the structure. Physical depreciation is brought about only by deterioration or condition of the element. If the objectionable colored paint was peeling and in poor condition, physical deterioration is occurring.

This scenario leads to another topic which should be understood—potential of double-counting depreciation. In the case of the objectionable paint color, if the paint were deteriorating and the entire house needed to be painted, a more acceptable color could be applied. Therefore, curing the physical deterioration is simultaneously curing the functional obsolescence. Thus, no functional depreciation should be applied.

There are times when it may be difficult to ascertain whether depreciation is caused by functional obsolescence or external obsolescence. It is important to understand the root cause of depreciation, so it can be properly categorized and determined to be curable or incurable; for example, a small convenience store whose business has slowly declined over time. Eventually, the owner is not able to command as much rent as before when the lease is up for renewal. The appraiser must determine the cause of this depreciation.

- Is business down because the building or property is too old or too small?
- Do customers perceive that the store is too small so as not to carry everything they might want?
- Is the parking lot too small?
- Is it because the store does not have a drive-thru like some of its competitors?

All of these factors would represent functional obsolescence that may or may not be curable. On the other hand:

- Is business down because there are now more competitors in the area?
- Are there new traffic patterns that make the store less convenient?
- Is the surrounding market area shrinking as people move to newer suburbs?

All of these would represent external obsolescence that is most likely incurable.

In the first set of circumstances where the obsolescence is functional, the appraiser must gauge the cost to improve the property to bring it in line with the demands of the marketplace. Once the appraiser determines this cost, then the analysis can be made about whether or not the deficiency is curable. In the second set of circumstances where the obsolescence is external, there is little that can be done to improve the value of the property as it is in its current state. The appraiser must then consider whether or not there is another highest and best use for the property.

One way to determine whether the perceived obsolescence is functional or external is for the appraiser to consider the land as if vacant and available for any use. By going through the exercise to determine the highest and best use for the property, the appraiser is also able to determine the cause of any obsolescence and the impact that it may have on value. In this way, the appraiser can see if the factors involved in the loss of value are affecting the site or only the structure.

The appraiser is trying to determine if the land is worth less because of factors in the marketplace, or if the structure is worth less because of factors in the marketplace. Would the site be worth more with a fast food location on it instead of the convenience store that is there now? If so, then the structure can be cited for the loss in value and attribute the loss to functional obsolescence. Or would the site be worth the same regardless of what type of structure or business is put there? If so, then the site location is the root cause for the loss in value to the property, and the loss in value is attributable to external obsolescence.

Impact of Depreciation on Property Value

In addition to quantifying any downward impact on value attributable to depreciation, there are a few other points that the appraiser must consider. Most of these require good judgment and logic on the part of the appraiser but are important because they influence the perception of buyers in the marketplace. Already discussed is how curb appeal can influence residential buyers without a direct correlation to depreciation. These buyers can see that a property with better upkeep will likely need less maintenance. Often buyers do not arithmetically calculate the differences between two properties.

Example

> Typical buyers may not look at property A and see that the house has new paint that should last 10 years. These same buyers, however, might look at property B and see that the house has paint that is five years old and conclude it will need new paint in five more years. Then from this, the buyer could calculate that having the house painted would cost $6,000, so property B should be priced $3,000 less, and continue this for each item in the property.

This may or may not represent the mind-set of residential buyers.

There are some residential properties being purchased by most owner-occupants in which differences in depreciation levels that do not need immediate attention nor rise to the level of severe deferred maintenance generally do not have a major impact on value. It would not be uncommon for property A and property B to be about the same price. It would also not be uncommon for property A to be more marketable and sell more quickly because of its perceived depreciation advantage, but the advantage is not quantified into a specific value difference.

With commercial or investment properties, the reality is almost the opposite of the previously described situation.. Although investors may not have another similar property, which they can readily purchase as a substitute, they are often meticulous about quantifying the cost of potential depreciation issues. In fact, a typical investor will require a lower price—and hence a higher return on an investment—for properties that have depreciation issues because higher levels of depreciation have the potential to shorten the useful or economic life of an investment property.

Estimating Depreciation

There are four methods of depreciation that will be discussed in this section:

1. Age-life method
2. Breakdown method
3. Market extraction method
4. Modified age-life method

Age-Life Method

The **age-life method** *estimates depreciation as a ratio of the effective age of improvements to the total economic life*. This is also called economic age-life method. The effective age of a structure is based on both physical and economic concepts. Deterioration is a physical concept while obsolescence is an economic concept. The effective age addresses all forms of depreciation by considering the presence of physical deterioration, functional obsolescence, and external obsolescence. The determination of a structure's effective age is heavily reliant on an appraiser's judgment and experience. Keep in mind, a building's effective age is not necessarily equal to its actual age.

Physically, maintenance and upkeep can lengthen a building's useful life and neglect can shorten it. When a property is renovated or repaired, the effective age becomes less and remaining economic life is lengthened.

Functionally, when design and functional elements of the improvements do not meet current market standards (such as an odd floor plan), the obsolescence will be reflected in the effective age.

Externally, if an undesirable element is present outside the subject property boundaries and is negatively affecting the subject property, the condition will be considered in the subject's effective age.

Example

To calculate age-life depreciation, a simple formula is used, whereby the effective age of the building is used and is divided by total expected life of the building to arrive at a total depreciation amount as a percentage.

Determine the depreciation of a $500,000 building using effective age-life depreciation. When built, the building had an expected economic life of 50 years. Its current effective age is 10 years old. Given these facts, calculate the building's depreciation.

Effective Age ÷ Total Expected Economic Life = Depreciation Percentage

10 ÷ 50 = 0.20 = 20%

So, **$500,000 × 20% = $100,000** (depreciation)

It is true that in many residential appraisals, physical deterioration will be the only element addressed in determining effective age. If that is the case, the owners of a well-maintained building can continue to get more useful economic life out of it. In fact, a well-kept building could remain at the same effective age for several years if it is properly maintained and kept to modern standards. Likewise, a building with significant deferred maintenance may demonstrate an effective age greater than its actual age. It may be better to tear down this kind of building rather than invest money to fix it.

Advantages to using the age-life method are that it is relatively simple, and the effects of different causes of depreciation are not as likely to be double counted. For example, if some component of the property is functionally obsolete and also worn out, replacing it would also eliminate the functional obsolescence. The main disadvantage with using the age-life method is there can be many variables in establishing the effective age. It is not always a simple case of wear and tear. The age-life method is the most commonly applied depreciation technique in residential appraisal. When a more detailed analysis is required by the scope of work, other methods of depreciation might be used.

Breakdown Method

The **breakdown method** is also sometimes called the **observed depreciation** method for determining observable depreciation. The breakdown method is much more complex than age-life, but it can be used along with the age-life method and the market extraction method as it assigns the total depreciation into the three categories we've discussed—physical deterioration, functional obsolescence, and external obsolescence. *This is accomplished by the appraiser's inspection of the structure, study of demographics, and analysis of the market or other external conditions.*

An appraiser must define the three causes of depreciation and must also consider whether the condition is curable or incurable.

Physical Deterioration

An appraiser estimates depreciation for physical deterioration by taking the new price of the item and subtracting a percentage for the deterioration present. The determination of an appropriate depreciation percentage requires judgment and experience on the appraiser's part. This calculation is easier for physical items, like a roof or a furnace. Here is a simple example.

Example

The furnace in a house cost $5,000 when it was new. Based on the appraiser's judgment, the furnace's current condition indicates about 20% of its life has been used. The useful remaining life of the furnace is 80%. So, to estimate the amount of depreciation attributed to that item:

$5,000 × 0.20 (20%) = $1,000 for furnace depreciation

This example illustrates depreciation for items that may need to be repaired at some point. If the item being inspected must be replaced, then the appraiser uses the current cost of replacing the item with a new one as the depreciation.

The test for deciding if physical deterioration is curable or incurable is quite simple. If the cost to repair or replace an item exceeds the value the repair would add to the property value, then the physical deterioration is said to be incurable. The contributory value of the item to be repaired or replaced must be considered. This does not necessarily mean the item should not be cured, but it does provide a basis for deciding whether it is worth the time, effort, and money to repair a property's shortcomings. Return on investment for money spent may also be taken into consideration. For extensive repairs, the time needed to complete the repairs and the time value of money are additional considerations that can complicate the calculations and the decision.

Functional Obsolescence

This cause of depreciation is observable during an inspection, but it may sometimes need confirmation with a demographics study or market analysis. A depreciation estimate for functional obsolescence is determined differently depending on whether the undesirable feature is curable or incurable. If the obsolescence is curable, then depreciation is equal to the cost of curing the undesirable feature. If the undesirable feature is incurable, then the appraiser estimates depreciation through paired data analysis, comparing sale prices of properties with the feature and without, and determining an adjustment for the undesirable feature.

When using replacement as a basis of cost for an existing structure, an important point is that replacement cost will cure most forms of functional obsolescence of the present structure. Thus, the appraiser must be cautious not to apply functional obsolescence when it has already been cured in the cost. Reproduction cost, however, reproduces the functional obsolescence, since the definition implies duplication. Functional obsolescence would need to be estimated.

Of course, when the improvement is new, given there is no obsolescence of the design or functional layout, replacement and reproduction are the same.

External Obsolescence

A depreciation estimate for external obsolescence is determined by a market analysis or through extraction using paired data analysis, comparing the difference in sale prices from a property with the external obsolescence and a similar property without it. That value difference observed from market data becomes the adjustment figure used in the appraisal.

Market Extraction Method

The **market extraction method** *is a technique for determining depreciation based on comparable sales of similar properties.* This method is sometimes called the **sales comparison method**, the **market comparison method**, or the **abstraction method**. The steps for extracting depreciation using this method are as follows:

- Identify comparable sold properties that share as many traits as possible with the subject.
- Make Adjustments to the comparable properties for conditions and significant differences, just like in the sales comparison approach.
- Subtract an amount for the market value of the site from the adjusted sale price of the comparable; this isolates the improvement value.
- Calculate the cost of building a replacement structure on the day the comparable property sold. (Cost manuals would be one way to accomplish this.)
- Take the replacement cost new for the improvement minus the amount extracted for the current improvement contribution and this will result in the amount of depreciation attributed to the improvement.

Total Market Value – Site Value = Improvement Contribution to

Value Replacement Cost New – Improvement Contribution =

Depreciation Amount

Example

Total Market Value
– Site Value

Improvement Contribution to Value

Replacement Cost New
– Improvement Contribution

Depreciation Amount

Market Extraction Method

\$310,000
– \$40,000

\$270,000

\$295,000
– \$270,000

\$25,000 Depreciation

If the improved and vacant land data is more comparable, then the market extraction method will be more reliable. Accuracy is also critical in developing the replacement cost for the comparable property.

As was mentioned earlier in this chapter, the market extraction method is also useful for indicating the economic or remaining economic life of a structure.

Example

A 25-year-old home sold for \$150,000. Sales comparison data for this market reveals that the site is worth about \$40,000. The replacement cost new for the home is \$160,000. The effective age of the home is 25 years.

Total Market Value – Site Value = Improvement Contribution to Value

\$150,000 – \$40,000 = \$110,000

Replacement Cost New – Improvement Contribution = Depreciation Amount

\$160,000 – \$110,000 = \$50,000

Depreciation Amount ÷ Effective Age = Annual Depreciation Amount

\$50,000 ÷ 25 = \$2,000

Replacement Cost New ÷ Annual Depreciation Amount = Total Economic Life

\$160,000 ÷ \$2,000 = 80

Total Economic Life – Effective Age = Remaining Economic Life

80 – 25 = 55

The remaining economic life of the home is 55 years.

Modified Effective Age-Life Method

A twist to the age-life method and the breakdown method of depreciation is the **modified age-life method**. This method can be employed when the curable depreciation is attributable to obsolescence for which the depreciation can be readily recognized and calculated. *The method takes the dollar amount to cure certain items, when the cost to cure is known.* Once the appraiser subtracts the cost to cure the curable items from the cost new and applies the age-life depreciation to the remaining cost (as if the items were cured), this will determine incurable depreciation. Total depreciation attributed to curable items and incurable items is added together to indicate total depreciation.

- **Step 1**: Identify depreciation due to curable items
- **Step 2**: Subtract the cost to cure curable items from the cost new of the structure
- **Step 3**: Apply age-life depreciation to the cost new minus cost of curable items to estimate depreciation due to incurable items
- **Step 4**: Add depreciation for curable items (cost to cure) and the depreciation due to incurable items to find the total depreciation

Example

The roof on a structure is estimated to have an effective age of 10 years. The economic life of the roof is 20 years. So, the roof is 50% depreciated. If the cost of the roof were $5,000, the depreciation would be $2,500.

- **10 ÷ 20 = 50%**
- **$5,000 x 50% = $2,500** Depreciation Attributable to Curable Items

The replacement cost new of the structure is $100,000. Therefore, the curable depreciation is subtracted from the cost new to leave a base (remaining cost new) for age-life deprecation of incurable items.

- **$100,000 – $2,500 = $97,500** Remaining Cost New

If the effective age (if the roof were new) of the structure is 20 years and remaining economic life of the structure is 60 years, the depreciation would be 25%

- **20 ÷ 80 = 25%**
- **$97,500 × 25% = $24,375** Depreciation Due to Incurable Items

Adding the depreciation from curable items (roof) $2,500 to the depreciation from incurable items, $24,375 will equal the total depreciation which would be $26,875.

- **$2,500 + $24,875 = $26,875** Total Depreciation Due to Curable and Incurable Items

Addressing Deficiencies and Superadequacies

Observed as a functional obsolescence, a deficiency can be deemed curable or incurable. When the deficiency is incurable, the functional depreciation due to the deficiency looks to the cost of the feature if it were included in the original construction versus the cost to add the feature presently.

Example

Every house on the street has an attached garage except the subject. However, there is ample room on the lot to add a garage. Market data suggests the subject is worth \$15,000 less than its competing neighborhood homes, directly due to the lack of a garage. A recent estimate to add a garage to the existing house was \$10,000. Therefore, the lack of a garage is curable because it will add more value than it will cost to build. If the garage could be built today in concert with the construction of the house, it would cost only \$8,000. The amount of functional depreciation due to the deficiency would be \$2,000—the difference between what it would cost if it were installed along with the original construction and the cost to add one after the fact.

A functional depreciation for a deficiency that is incurable is handled much the same. Using the previous example, loss in value due to the lack of a garage is \$15,000. The incurable functional depreciation due to the incurable deficiency would be the difference between the loss in value and the cost if installed new.

\$15,000 (Loss in Value)
– \$8,000 (Cost if Installed New)
= \$ 7,000

Another method for calculating the loss in value to a property as a component of the analysis of a deficiency, when the subject property is an income producing property, relies on the income approach.

Example

A four-unit apartment building in a warm climate area has no central air-conditioning. Several industry professionals agree that due to the age and design of the property, installing central air-conditioning would be physically prohibitive. Market data supports that each unit rents for \$50 per month less than comparable units that have central air-conditioning. The appraiser determined that a GRM for the property is 125.

4 × \$50 = \$200 × 125 = \$25,000 Loss in Value

A **superadequacy** is *an item or feature that is greater than will be recognized by the market or is greater than is necessary for operation of the property*.

The formula for curable functional depreciation due to a superadequacy is as follows:

Cost to Remove the Superadequate Item
– Salvage Value
+ Cost to Install a Market Acceptable (or Correct) Item
= Curable Functional Depreciation Due to a Superadequacy

Incurable depreciation due to a superadequacy is most often related to the loss in income due to the superadequacy or market reaction in terms of dollars.

Remember: Replacement costs are typically used to eliminate the need for depreciating superadequacies and deficiencies.

Final Indication of Value via the Cost Approach

In the final step of the cost approach, various components, which have been discussed in this text, come together to produce a final indication of value. There is only one final element that needs to be reviewed that is typically associated with most cost analysis—the as-is value of "other" site improvements.

"Other" Site Improvements

If the scope of work in an assignment requires a detailed analysis, various miscellaneous site improvements might be specified with a cost new with appropriate depreciation (if any) applied. This is often the technique in keeping with the scope of work for proposed construction. However, for existing properties, most often the contributory value of other site improvements will be considered "as-is" or in their depreciated state. In other words, considered on an as-is basis, the contributory value is already depreciated and must not be included in the cost new and subject to additional depreciation along with the structure.

Included improvement elements not already considered in the cost calculations are:

- Driveways
- Landscaping
- Walkways
- Utility provisions

In their as-is state, a contributory value of other improvements is stated as an aggregate dollar amount as of the effective date of the appraisal.

Final Cost Approach Analysis

The cost approach is a valuation method that develops an opinion of value for a property by calculating the cost of building the structure on the land, subtracting any depreciation, and adding in the value of the site and any other miscellaneous site improvements. STANDARDS 1–4 of the Uniform Standards of Professional Appraisal Practice (USPAP) states, when a cost approach is necessary for credible assignment results, an appraiser must develop an opinion of site value by an appropriate appraisal method, analyze such comparable cost data as are available to estimate the cost new of the improvements, and analyze such comparable cost data as are available to estimate the difference between cost new and the present worth of the improvements—depreciation.

The steps in the final cost approach analysis consistent with the scope of work in the assignment include:

- Definition of the basis for the cost
- Reproduction
- Replacement

A costing method is chosen and a cost new is developed:

- Comparative unit
- Quantity survey
- Unit-in-place
- Index

Depreciation is estimated to address physical deterioration, functional obsolescence, and external obsolescence of the structure(s) using one of the following recognized methods:

- Age-life
- Market extraction
- Breakdown
- Modified age-life method

As-is contributory value of other site improvements is added (e.g., utilities, driveway, landscaping).

Vacant land value, developed by accepted methods and based on the land's highest and best use, is added.

Conclude an opinion of value.

Now that the various components of research, analysis and development required for the cost approach have been discussed, the only thing left to do is to put it all together to indicate a value conclusion. Here we see a simple cost approach.

Cost Approach Sample

Replacement Cost of House	2,400 Square Feet X $102.00 Per Square Foot = $244,800		
Depreciation (Physical)	Effective Age Remaining Economic Life 15 years ÷ 70 years (15 + 55) = 21.4286% Depreciation $244,800 x 21.4286% = $52,457 (rounded) $244,800 – $52,457 =	15 years 55 years	**$192,343**
Site Value	$38,000		
Other Site Improvements	$10,000		
Indicated Value by the Cost Approach	**$240,343**		

Reporting the Cost Approach

The final reporting of the cost approach may be presented in various styles consistent with the reporting option chosen and the intended use and user(s) of the appraisal. As well, when using different appraisal reporting forms, their presentation may vary.

In most cases of residential appraisals used for mortgage finance transactions, the cost approach will be reported on one of the Fannie Mae/Freddie Mac Forms. The illustration below is an excerpt from the Uniform Residential Appraisal Report (URAR) form prescribed by Fannie Mae and Freddie Mac and adopted by many other mortgage lending entities for use, as well.

COST APPROACH TO VALUE (not required by Fannie Mae)

Provide adequate information for the lender/client to replicate the below cost figures and calculations.

Support for the opinion of site value (summary of comparable land sales or other methods for estimating site value) ESTIMATED SITE VALUE IS DERIVED FROM A SALES COMPARISON ANALYSIS OF LOT SALES WITHIN THE SUBJECT'S SUBDIVISION. THIS ANALYSIS IS CONTAINED IN THE APPRAISER'S WORKFILE.

COST APPROACH		
ESTIMATED ☐ REPRODUCTION OR ☒ REPLACEMENT COST NEW	OPINION OF SITE VALUE	=$ 35,000
Source of cost data MARSHALL SWIFT COSTING SERVICE	DWELLING 1,952 Sq.Ft. @ $ 67.40	=$ 131,565
Quality rating from cost service AVG Effective date of cost data 3/1/2005	FOUNDATION 642 Sq.Ft. @ $ 12.00	=$ 7,704
Comments on Cost Approach (gross living area calculations, depreciation, etc.)		=$
GROSS LIVING AREA HAS BEEN DETERMINED FROM EXTERIOR	Garage/Carport 528 Sq.Ft. @ $ 18.00	=$ 9,504
DIMENSIONS. LOCAL COST DATA CONTAINED IN THE	Total Estimate of Cost-New	=$ 148,773
APPRAISER'S FILES HAS ALSO BEEN RESEARCHED.	Less Physical / Functional / External	
DEPRECIATION HAS BEEN CALCULATED USING THE AGE/LIFE	Depreciation 5,951	=$(5,951)
METHOD.	Depreciated Cost of Improvements	=$ 142,822
	"As-is" Value of Site Improvements	=$ 5,000
Estimated Remaining Economic Life (HUD and VA only) 72 Years	INDICATED VALUE BY COST APPROACH	=$ 182,822

It should be noted that while some lenders may require, as an assignment condition, that the cost approach be developed and reported, the method is not required in most circumstances by Fannie Mae or Freddie Mac.

Using the Cost Approach

The cost approach provides a very reliable tool for determining a value for replacing or reproducing buildings, especially when the improvements are new or nearly new. For single use or special purpose buildings for which there is a scarcity or lack of relevant comparable or income data, the cost approach is usually the primary method of developing an opinion of value. The use of the cost approach is often critical in a highest and best use analysis. Observing the theory of substitution, the cost approach can provide a ceiling or upper end of value by which to support an opinion concluded by other appraisal methods. However, the cost approach can often be complex and sometimes difficult when applied to older buildings that suffer from physical deterioration and functional or external obsolescence, and, therefore, confidence in the method may diminish. Finally, typical and informed buyers usually do not base a purchase or investment decision on cost when considering the purchase of existing, improved real estate in an established neighborhood.

Work Problems

1. Indicate which type of depreciation the problem reflects in the appropriate column to the right.

Problem	Physical Deterioration	Functional Obsolescence	External Obsolescence
Broken handrail on stairs			
Railway tracks at back of property			
House in approach zone to major airport			
Water-stained ceiling			
Missing exterior shutter			
Bath with toilet, tub, and no sink			
Hole in drywall			
24-inch doorways into bedrooms			
Only bath accessed through a bedroom			
Second floor has no heat			

2. The cost new of a dwelling has been estimated at $137,000. The estimated cost identified for curable items is $4,300. Once cured, the dwelling is estimated to have an effective age of 15 years with a remaining economic life of 65 years. What is the amount of incurable depreciation once all curable items are cured?

3. The age-life method is being used in the cost approach to depreciate a single-family residence. The site value has been determined at $37,000, and the "as is" value of "other" site improvements at $6,500. Reproduction costs have been broken down as follows:

   - $77 per square foot for the 700-square-foot, two-story main house
   - $82 per square foot for the one-story family room addition containing 370 square feet
   - $13 per square foot for the basement under the main house
   - $18.50 per square foot for the attached two-car garage, which is 24′ × 26′

   The effective age of the main house is 35 years with a remaining economic life of 45 years. The one-story addition and attached garage have an effective age of 10 years and a remaining economic life of 55 years.

   A. What is the GLA of the house?

   B. What is the reproduction cost new of the entire structure?

   C. What is the percent of depreciation to the main house?

   D. What is the percent of depreciation to the family room addition and garage?

   E. What is the overall rate of depreciation?

   F. What is the indication of value by the cost approach?

4. Using the breakdown method, calculate the depreciation of a roof that cost $7,500 and has about 10% left of its life.

5. An improved property is currently valued at $173,000. From market data, the site is worth $42,000. The effective age is 20 years. Replacement cost of the house is $185,000. Using the market extraction method, find the total economic life of the subject house.

SUMMARY

1. **Depreciation** is a monetary loss in value of property for any reason. Depreciation is only applied to the structure on the land and other site improvements. **Accrued depreciation** is the difference between the current value of an improvement and the cost of replacing the improvement. The three forces that cause depreciation are physical deterioration, functional obsolescence, and external obsolescence. The effective age of a structure is based on all forces of deterioration and obsolescence and considers a structure's physical condition, how acceptably functional a structure is, and the external factors that influence a structure.
2. **Economic life** is the time during which a structure can generate more income than operating expenses cost and is a reflection of all three of the forces of depreciation. **Useful life** relates to the period of time a structure or a component of the structure can be expected to function for the purpose it was designed for and relates only to physical deterioration. Remaining economic life references the period of usefulness a structure has remaining as of the effective date of the appraisal. The total economic life of a structure is comprised by the total of the effective age and the remaining economic life.
3. **Physical deterioration** and **functional obsolescence** is classified as either curable or incurable. If the cost to cure exceeds the value that is added to the property value, the condition is incurable. If the cost to cure is less than the contributory value added to the property, the condition is curable. For physical deterioration, the deteriorated elements are categorized further as short-lived or long-lived items.
4. An **underimprovement** is when the improvements do not conform to the highest and best use of the site, thus the property does not achieve maximum value. An overimprovement is a non-conformity where the improvements and likewise the cost of the improvements exceed the completed market value.
5. A **deficiency** is when a feature or component of a property is inadequate in the marketplace and results in a loss of market value. A **superadequacy** is when a feature or component of a property is too large, too expensive, or of too high a quality such that its cost exceeds the contributory value of that item or feature.
6. Four common **methods of depreciation** include the age-life method, breakdown method, market extraction method, and the modified age-life method.
7. The **cost approach** is a valuation method that develops an opinion of value for a property by calculating the cost of building the structure on the land, subtracting any depreciation, and adding in the value of the site and any other miscellaneous site improvements.

QUIZ

1. ***A building's age, based on all forms of obsolescence and deterioration, is referred to as its***
   a. actual age.
   b. depreciation.
   c. economic life.
   d. effective age.

2. ***The period of usefulness that a structure has left as of the effective date of the appraisal is referred to as***
   a. chronological effective age.
   b. market extraction depreciation.
   c. remaining economic life.
   d. straight-line method.

3. ***An appraiser is developing the cost approach of a seven-month-old home in a new subdivision. The one story home is built on a concrete slab that is 55 feet by 40 feet, which includes 500 square feet of built-in garage area. Cost indications are $5 per square foot for the concrete slab, $45 per square foot for the garage, and $81 per square foot for the living area. What is the total cost new for the home?***
   a. $160,700
   b. $171,200
   c. $201,700
   d. $211,700

4. ***A structure has an expected economic life of 100 years and an effective age of 20 years. If the building cost new is $500,000, what is the depreciation amount?***
   a. $100,000
   b. $200,000
   c. $300,000
   d. $400,000

5. ***What is deferred maintenance usually classified as?***
   a. curable external obsolescence
   b. curable physical deterioration
   c. incurable functional obsolescence
   d. incurable physical deterioration

6. ***A building has a total expected economic life of 75 years and an effective age of 25 years. If the replacement cost is $750,000, what is the current value of the building?***
   a. $187,500
   b. $250,000
   c. $500,000
   d. $562,500

7. ***What is the primary consideration in determining whether depreciation is curable?***
   a. cost of repairs
   b. functional vs. external
   c. number of items needing repair
   d. reserve replacement fund

8. ***An office building with older carpet is worth $750,000. If the carpet is replaced, the building is still worth $750,000. When considering value, the carpet should***
   a. be replaced because that is expected for short-lived items.
   b. be replaced to make the property sell faster.
   c. not be replaced because it is incurable, short-lived depreciation item.
   d. not be replaced because it is a long-lived depreciation item.

9. ***Calculate the observable depreciation of this short-lived building component in a residential dwelling.***

   Component—floor coverings
   Cost new of floor coverings $7,200
   Remaining life of floor coverings 60%
   Market value of dwelling $167,000

   a. $1,238
   b. $2,880
   c. $3,096
   d. $4,320

10. ***A house with outdated 1960's electrical fixtures is worth $425,000. An appraiser determines that spending $25,000 on new fixtures would make the house worth $475,000. This is an example of***

a. curable short-lived.
b. economic obsolescence.
c. replacement cost.
d. superadequacy.

11. ***An appraiser's scope of work includes allocating depreciation by percentages to physical, functional, and external causes. The property has an effective age of 10 years with a remaining economic life of 40 years. Physical depreciation is 7% and functional depreciation is 5%. What is percent is external depreciation?***

a. 8%
b. 17%
c. 20%
d. 25%

12. ***What would be the total depreciation applied if curing the functional obsolescence would simultaneously eliminate all physical deterioration?***

Depreciation due to functional obsolescence—$1,000
Depreciation due to physical deterioration—$400

a. $400
b. $600
c. $1,000
d. $1,400

13. ***A property requires exterior paint at a cost of $10,000. New carpet, interior paint, and bath and kitchen fixtures will cost $17,500. Once these items are cured, the structure will have an effective age of 15 years and remaining economic life of 45 years. If the reproduction cost new of the dwelling is $230,000, what is the total depreciation using the modified age-life method?***

a. $64,730
b. $71,375
c. $78,125
d. $85,000

14. ***What is the period of time a building can be useful and generate more than is paid out in expenses?***

a. allocated life
b. economic life
c. effective life
d. productive life

15. ***What is the value indicated by the cost approach?***

Site value—$32,000
Dwelling size—2,250 square feet
Replacement cost—$87.42 per square feet
Garage—576 square feet
Replacement cost—$16.00 per square feet
As-is value of site improvements—$6,000
Effective age—5 years
Remaining economic life—75 years

a. $223,041.56
b. $225,041.56
c. $229,041.56
d. $231,041.56

Glossary

The definitions given here explain how the listed terms are used in the real estate appraisal field. Some terms have additional meanings, which can be found in a standard dictionary.

Abandonment The failure to occupy and use property, which may result in a loss of rights.

Absorption Analysis A study to determine how many property units can be sold or rented in the marketplace during a certain period of time.

Absorption Period The period of time it will take a property unit to be sold or rented in the marketplace.

Abstract of Title A brief, chronological summary of the recorded documents affecting the title to a particular parcel of real property.

Acceptance 1. Agreeing to the terms of an offer to enter into a contract, thereby creating a binding contract. 2. Taking delivery of a deed.

Access A means of entry to a property.

Accession The acquisition of title to land by its addition to real estate already owned, through human actions or natural processes.

Accretion A gradual addition to dry land by the forces of nature, mostly used for property abutting a body of water where such addition is made by the deposits of waterborne sediment carried by rivers, winds, tides, etc. to the shoreline property.

Accrued Depreciation The total accumulated depreciation.

Ad Valorem A Latin phrase meaning "according to value," used to refer to taxes assessed on the value of real property.

Addenda Additional parts of an appraisal report. Addenda usually consist of photos of the subject improvements and comparable properties, a sketch of the subject's floor plan, a table for calculating the area of the subject, a location map, or additional necessary comments.

Adjustable Rate Mortgage A mortgage that permits the lender to periodically adjust the interest rate to reflect fluctuations in the cost of money. Also called **ARM**.

Adjusted Sale Price The final, estimated price of a comparable property after all additions and subtractions have been made for differences between the comparable and the subject.

Advocacy Representing the cause or interest of another, even if that cause or interest does not necessarily coincide with one's own beliefs, opinions, conclusions, or recommendations.

Age-Life Depreciation A calculation that takes the effective age of a property and divides it by the total economic life.

Air Rights The right to undisturbed use and control of the airspace over a parcel of land, within reasonable limits for air travel. Air rights may be transferred separately from the land.

Alienation Clause A contract clause that gives the lender certain stated rights when a transfer of property ownership takes place. Upon the sale of, or even transfer of, significant interest in the property, the lender often has the right to accelerate the debt, change the interest rate, or charge a hefty assumption fee. FHA and VA loans cannot contain this clause.

Allocation Method A site valuation method that separates the value of the land from the structures that sit on it by taking a ratio of the land or site value to the total property value, based on a typical property in the area.

Amenity A tangible or intangible feature that enhances and adds value to real estate.

Amortization Elimination of a debt with a series of equal payments (principal and interest) at regular time intervals.

Anchor Tenant The main store in a shopping center, expected to draw the most people.

Annexation Attaching personal property to land so the law views it as part of real property.

Annexer A person who owns an item as personal property and brings it onto real property, making it a part of the real property.

ANSI American National Standards Institute; responsible for GLA standards.

Anticipation An economic theory that says value is created by the expectation of future benefits, such as profit, pleasure, tax shelter, production, income, etc.

Appraisal The act or process of developing an opinion of value; an opinion of value of or pertaining to appraising and related functions, such as appraisal practice or appraisal services.

Appraisal Foundation A nonprofit private organization which is recognized by Congress as the authority for professional appraisal standards and appraiser qualifications.

Appraisal Review The act or process of developing and communicating an opinion about the quality of another appraiser's work that was performed as part of an appraisal or appraisal review assignment.

Appraiser One who is expected to perform valuation services competently and in a manner that is independent, impartial, and objective.

Appreciation An increase to the value of property.

Appropriative Rights Water rights allocated by government permit, according to an appropriation system. It is not necessary to own property beside the body of water to apply for an appropriation permit.

Appurtenance A right that goes with ownership of real property. It is usually transferred with the property but may be sold separately. This is a legal term referring to both physical and nonphysical appurtenances.

Arm's Length Transaction A transaction that occurred under typical conditions in the marketplace, with each of the parties acting in their own best interests.

"As Is" Clause A provision in a purchase agreement stating that the buyer accepts the property in its present condition.

Assemblage The combining of two or more parcels of land into one larger parcel.

Assessment 1. A government's valuation of property for tax purposes. 2. A special tax, usually used to pay for community improvements.

Assessment Ratio The ratio of a property's tax assessed value to its market value.

Assessor An official who determines the value of property for taxation.

Assignment A valuation service provided as a consequence of an agreement between an appraiser and a client; the valuation service provided as a result of an agreement.

Assignment Results An appraiser's opinions and conclusions developed specific to an assignment.

Assumption That which is taken to be true.

Attachment 1. Things connected to the land, whether natural or man-made. Man-made attachments are called improvements. 2. Court-ordered seizure of property belonging to a defendant in a lawsuit so it will be available to satisfy a judgment. In the case of real property, attachment creates a lien.

Attachments, Natural Things growing on land, such as trees, shrubs, or crops.

Balance 1. A condition that exists in the real estate market when there are slightly more homes available than buyers. 2. The right mix of capital, entrepreneurship/management, labor, and land (the four agents of production) that results in best return on investment from land. Highest and best use occurs when the four agents of production are in balance.

Balloon (Framing) A type of framing with long studs up the entire length of the house, from the foundation to the roof. No longer permitted as a construction method by most building codes.

Base Companies Companies and industries that bring new business and jobs to an area.

Base Lines Primary east-west lines designated and named throughout the country for use with the government survey system.

Base Multiplier A number used to show how many service (non-basic) jobs are affected by one base job.

Basement Part of a house or building that is partially or entirely below grade (ground level), and is used to support the rest of the structure.

Bias A preference or inclination that precludes an appraiser's impartiality, independence, or objectivity in an assignment.

Bill of Sale A document used to transfer title to personal property from one person to another.

Blue Prints Detailed building plans used to evaluate design, determine feasibility, and guide construction of a structure.

Boundary 1. The perimeter or border of a parcel of land. 2. The dividing line between one piece of property and another.

Break Even The amount of operating income needed to pay operating expenses and debt service.

Breakdown Method A method for calculating depreciation by taking a figure for each kind of depreciation and combining them into one number.

BTU (British Thermal Unit) The amount of heat needed to raise the temperature of one pound of water by one degree Fahrenheit. It is used as a measure of furnace or air conditioner capacity.

Building Code A means of setting construction standards, requiring builders to use particular methods and materials; regulations establishing minimum standards for construction and materials. (There are different building codes for different systems: Electric, plumbing, etc.)

Building Inspection A process whereby local government employees, often engineers, are charged with ensuring compliance with state and local building codes.

Building Permits Official documents from a local government or other authority that allow the beginning of a construction or remodeling project.

Bundle of Rights All real property rights conferred with ownership including, but not limited to, right of use, right of enjoyment, and right of disposal.

Business Cycles General swings in business, resulting in expanding and contracting activity during different phases of the cycle.

Buydown When additional funds, in the form of points, are paid to a lender at the beginning of a loan to lower the interest rate and monthly payments on the loan.

Buyer's Market A situation in the real estate market where buyers have a large selection of properties from which to choose.

Capitalization of Ground Rents Method A site valuation method that takes an estimated value of improvements and subtracts it from the total sales price to derive a figure for the land value.

Cash Equivalency Adjustment An adjustment applied to the sale price of a comparable sale, to address atypical financing terms.

Caveat Emptor A Latin phrase meaning "let the buyer beware."

CC&Rs A declaration of covenants, conditions, and restrictions is placed on deeds by a developer or owner. The purpose of CC&Rs is to keep the subdivision attractive and protect the market value of homes. In most cases CC & Rs have a positive impact on value because they promote conformity in the neighborhood..

Change A principle affecting value in real estate that says all factors that influence real estate—physical, economic, governmental, and social—are constantly changing, and thus property value itself is subject to constant change.

Chattel A piece of personal property.

Civil Rights Fundamental humanitarian rights guaranteed to all persons by law.

Client The party or parties who engage an appraiser (by employment or contract) in a specific assignment.

Climate The weather conditions of a given area.

Closing The transfer of ownership of real property from seller to buyer, according to terms and conditions in sales contracts or escrow agreements. The final stage in a real estate transaction.

Closing Costs Expenses incurred in the transfer of real estate in addition to the purchase price; for example, the appraisal fee, title insurance premiums, broker's commission, and transfer tax.

Commercial Property Property zoned and used for business purposes, such as warehouses, restaurants, and office buildings, as distinguished from residential, industrial, or agricultural property.

Common Areas The land and improvements in a condominium, planned unit development, or cooperative that all residents use and own as tenants in common, such as the parking lot, hallways, and recreational facilities. These areas do not include individual apartment units or homes.

Comparables Similar properties that have sold recently in a certain area. Also called **Comps**.

Comparative Unit Method A method for determining the cost of a building that uses the cost of recently built comparable buildings as a basis for estimating the cost of replacing the subject property.

Competency Rule A USPAP Rule that requires appraisers to have knowledge and experience necessary to complete assignments competently, and also contains procedures for appraisers who do not have sufficient competence.

Competition Two or more parties, properties, etc., trying to obtain the same thing.

Competitive Supply Available properties that a buyer would accept as ready substitutes because they share the same features and utility as the subject.

Competitive Use A property that offers the same products or services as other properties in the immediate area, and thus will compete against them for customers.

Complementary Use A property that offers different products or services than other properties in the immediate area, and thus will benefit from the traffic and customers that patronize the other businesses.

Condemnation 1. Taking private property for public use through the government's power of eminent domain. Also called **Appropriation**. 2. A declaration that a structure is unfit for occupancy and must be closed or demolished.

Condition 1. Provisions in a deed or other document that make the parties' rights and obligations depend on the occurrence or non-occurrence of some event. 2. The state of repair or disrepair of an item, structure, etc.

Conditional Use A land use that does not comply with the general zoning rules for the zone in which it is located, but is permitted because it benefits the public (e.g., a hospital in a residential neighborhood). Also called **Special Exception**.

Condominium A property developed for co-ownership, where each co-owner has a separate interest in an individual unit and an undivided interest in the common areas of the property.

Conforming Loans Loans that meet qualifying standards, and thus can be sold on the secondary market.

Conformity The theory that says a particular property achieves its maximum value when it is surrounded by properties that are similar in style, function, and utility. Also called **Homogeneity**.

Construction Cost The dollar amount of material, labor, etc., required to build a structure.

Contract An agreement between two or more parties to do or not do a certain thing. The requirements for an enforceable contract are **capacity**, **mutual consent**, **lawful objective**, and **consideration**. In addition, certain contracts must be in writing to be enforceable.

Contract, Land A real estate installment agreement where the buyer makes payments to the seller in exchange for the right to occupy and use property. No deed or title is transferred until all, or a specified portion of, the payments have been made. Also called **Installment Land Contract**, **Installment Sales Contract**, **Land Sales Contract**, **Real Estate Contract**, and other names.

Contract Rent What tenants are actually paying in rent, as stated in the terms of the lease.

Contractor's Profit The profit earned by the manager of a construction project.

Contribution The theory that a particular item or feature of a property is only worth what it actually contributes in value to that parcel of real estate. This is known as the feature's **Contributory Value**.

Cooperative A building owned by a corporation, where the residents are shareholders in the corporation. Each shareholder receives a proprietary lease on an individual unit and the right to use the common areas.

Corner Influence The value change in a property because it sits on a corner lot.

Cost The dollars needed to develop, produce, or build something.

Cost Approach An appraisal method that estimates the value of real estate by establishing the cost new of replacing or reproducing the improvements, minus depreciation, plus the value of the site.

Cost Estimating Determining the price to replace or reproduce a structure.

Cost Inflation An increase in the cost of goods or services.

Cost Manuals—Books, electronic media, and online sources that give estimated construction costs for various types of buildings in different areas of the country.

Cost of Money The interest rate that people or businesses pay to use another's money for their own purposes.

Cost Services Companies that provide appraisers with accurate, up-to-date data on building costs for labor and materials.

Covenant 1. A contract. 2. A promise. 3. A guarantee (express or implied) in a document such as a deed or lease. 4. A restrictive covenant.

Covenant of Quiet Enjoyment A guarantee that a buyer or tenant has the right to exclusive, undisturbed possession of a leasehold estate, and will not be disturbed by the previous owner, the lessor, or anyone else claiming an interest in the property.

Crawl Space The unfinished space below the first floor of a house or other structure that is less than a full story in height.

Curable Repairable Repairable or able to be fixed; something that can be fixed at a reasonable cost with the value added to the property being more than the cost of the repair.

Curb Appeal The visual impression that buyers and others get from a property before entering it.

Data Information collected from various resources.

Days on Market (DOM) The amount of time a property is available for sale or lease.

Decline The third stage a neighborhood goes through in its life cycle, when property values begin to fall as demand falls.

Deed An instrument that conveys the grantor's interest in real property.

Deferred Maintenance Physical deterioration created when required repairs are ignored.

Deficiency Property element that is less than necessary, interpreted by the market to be unacceptable, or an element that is functionally inadequate.

Demand The need or desire for a specific good or service by others.

Demographic Data Information about the people in a given area.

Depreciate To decline in value.

Depreciation A loss in value to property for any reason—physical deterioration, functional obsolescence, external obsolescence.

Depreciation, External A loss in value from forces or elements outside the property's boundaries.

Depreciation, Functional A loss in value from design features that are no longer competitive with current market demands.

Depreciation, Observable Any loss of value the appraiser can attribute to physical deterioration, functional obsolescence, or economic obsolescence.

Depreciation, Physical A loss in value from deterioration of the physical structure or from deferred maintenance.

Direct Capitalization An income method that converts a property's single-year net operating income (NOI) into a value indication by applying an overall capitalization rate: NOI ÷ Overall Capitalization Rate = Value.

Direct Costs Costs in a project that are not variable, such as labor and materials. Also called **Hard Costs**.

Disaggregation A process that involves separating different users and different uses for property in the real estate market, focusing on real estate products on the supply side of the market.

Discount Points An amount paid to a lender when a loan is made to make up the difference between the current market interest rate and the rate a lender gives a borrower on a note. Discount points increase a lender's yield on a note, allowing the lender to give a borrower a lower interest rate.

Discount Rate The interest rate charged by the Federal Reserve Banks on loans to member commercial banks. Also called **Federal Discount Rate**.

Discrimination Treating people unequally because of race, religion, sex, national origin, age, or some other characteristic of a protected class, in violation of civil rights laws.

District The narrowest of definitions of a market area. A district is an area consisting of one particular land use, such as multi-family residential, commercial, industrial, etc.

Easement A right to use some part of another person's real property for a particular purpose. An easement is irrevocable and creates an interest in the property.

Easement, Appurtenant An easement that burdens one piece of land for the benefit of another.

Easement by Express Grant An easement granted to another in a deed or other document.

Easement by Express Reservation An easement created in a deed when a landowner is dividing property, transferring the servient tenement but retaining the dominant tenement.

Easement by Implication An easement created by operation of law instead of express grant or reservation when land is divided, if there is a long-standing, apparent use that is reasonably necessary for enjoyment of the dominant tenement. Also called **Implied Easement**.

Easement by Necessity A special kind of easement by implication that occurs when the dominant tenement would be completely useless without an easement, even if it is not a long-standing, apparent use.

Easement by Prescription An easement acquired by prescription. Also called **Prescriptive Easement**.

Easement in Gross An easement that benefits a person instead of a piece of land; there is a dominant tenant but no dominant tenement.

Economic Base The main business or industry in an area that a community uses to support and sustain itself.

Economic Base Analysis A study of the present business and employment situation in an area to determine the likelihood of continued stability, growth, or decline.

Economic Life The period of time, during the life of an improvement, over which the improvement contributes to the total property value.

Effective Age The age of a structure based on the actual wear and tear that the building shows from physical, functional, or external obsolescence; not necessarily the structure's age.

Effective Age-Life Method A simple depreciation method that divides the effective age by the economic life to reveal the percent of depreciation to be applied.

Effective Date The context for the appraiser's opinions and conclusions. Effective dates can be current, retrospective, or prospective.

Effective Demand The prospective buyer having enough disposable income available to satisfy his needs, wants, and desires. Also called **Effective Purchasing Power**.

Effective Gross Income (EGI) Potential gross income, less vacancy and collection losses.

Effective Gross Income Multiplier (EGIM) A factor derived and applied using EGI—the amount after estimated vacancy has been deducted from potential gross income (PGI).

Egress Means of exiting a property.

Electrical System A house system comprised of several elements, including such things as the wiring, distribution box, circuit breaker box, circuit breakers, fuses, lights and lighting fixtures, light switches, and wall outlets.

Elements of Comparison Characteristics of a property or a transaction that can be used to explain differences in the price paid in a transaction.

Eminent Domain The government's constitutional power to appropriate or condemn private property for public use, as long as the owner is paid just compensation. The government's taking of private land is called **Condemnation**. Condemnation is the *action*; eminent domain is the *right*.

Encroachment A physical object intruding onto neighboring property, often due to a mistake regarding the boundary.

Encumbrance A non-possessory interest in property; a lien, easement, or restrictive covenant, burdening the property owner's title.

Entrepreneurial Incentive A dollar value attributable for the expertise and efforts provided in the connection of the development, such as the entrepreneur's expertise, skills, and involvement with development (e.g., leasing, selling) of the project.

Entrepreneurial Profit A figure derived from the market representing an amount received by the entrepreneur for his contributions and risk accepted in a project.

Environmental Hazard A situation that exists in which there is potential for harm to persons or property from conditions that exist in a property or the surrounding area.

Environmental Impact Statement (EIS) A study required for all federal and federally related projects by the National Environmental Policy Act, which details a development project's impact on energy use, sewage systems, drainage, water facilities, schools, and other environmental, economic, and social areas.

Equity Yield Rate The rate of return on an investment, considering all income cash flow plus money invested in the property and eventual sale proceeds.

Escheat When property reverts to the state after a person dies without leaving a valid will and without heirs. Property also reverts to the state after abandonment.

Estate 1. A possessory interest in real property; either a freehold estate or a leasehold estate. 2. The real and personal property left by someone who has died.

Ethics Rule A USPAP Rule that (among other things) requires appraisers to avoid actions that could be considered misleading or fraudulent.

Excess Site Land or site area that is not necessary to support the use of the existing improvements situated on the subject property. However, it may have its own highest and best use for expansion of the current improvement or for sale for another use.

External Obsolescence When something outside the control of a property makes it less desirable. External obsolescence can be locational or economic.

Externalities Any event, item, etc., outside the boundaries of a property.

Extraction Method A site valuation method that takes an estimated value of improvements and subtracts it from the total sales price to derive a figure for the land value.

Extraordinary Assumption An assumption that a factor is true, directly related to a specific assignment, which could alter the appraisal's opinions or conclusions if found to be false.

Extrapolation Concluding outside (higher or lower) the known range of data.

Feasibility Analysis A study of the cost-benefit relationship of an economic endeavor. Also referred to as a **Feasibility Study**.

Fee An estate of inheritance; title to real property that can be willed or descend to heirs.

Fee Simple Absolute The greatest estate (ownership) one can have in real property; it is freely transferable and inheritable, and of indefinite duration, with no conditions on the title. Also called **Fee Simple** or **Fee Title**.

Financial Institutions Reform, Recovery and Enforcement Act (FIRREA) An act passed in 1989 as a comprehensive savings and loan bailout and preventive measure against future S&L insolvency. This act recognizes USPAP as the industry standard for appraisals, and identifies the Appraisal Foundation as the authority for professional appraisal standards.

Fiscal Policy The government's plan for spending, taxation, and debt management.

Fixed Expenses Ongoing operating expenses that do not vary based on occupancy levels of the property (e.g., taxes and insurance).

Fixture A man-made attachment; an item of personal property that has been attached to or closely associated with real property in such a way that it legally becomes part of the real property. Major fixtures are called **Improvements**.

Flashing Material used to cover joints where two or more different types of materials join together for the purpose of preventing water from penetrating the joint (e.g., metal over the seam between a brick chimney and a shingle roof).

Forecasting Creating future assumptions based on current data models and trends.

Foreclosure When a lienholder causes property to be sold so unpaid debt secured by the lien can be satisfied from the sale proceeds.

Foundation The basic structure on which the rest of the building will sit. A foundation can be **concrete slab**, **pier and beams**, **crawl spaces**, or **basement**.

Four Unities The unities of time, title, interest, and possession that are required for a joint tenancy.

Framing The basic load bearing skeleton of the house to which interior walls, exterior walls, and roof are attached. The framing can be **platform**, **post and beam**, or **balloon**.

Fraud An intentional or negligent misrepresentation or concealment of a material fact; making statements that a person knows, or should realize, are false or misleading.

Freehold A possessory interest in real property of uncertain (and often unlimited) duration; an ownership estate in real property, either a fee simple or life estate. The holder of a freehold estate has title.

Frontage The dimension across the access side of a parcel of land (usually along the road). When a lot size is stated, the first number is the lot frontage.

Fructus Industriales Plants planted and cultivated by people ("fruits of industry").

Fructus Naturales Naturally occurring plants ("fruits of nature").

Fully Amortized Loans Loans in which the total payments over the life of the loan will pay off the entire balance of principal and interest due at the end of the loan term.

Functional Obsolescence When a building is less desirable because of something inherent in the design of the structure.

Functional Utility When a building has the adequate design and features to be used as intended.

Future Value The worth of something at some later point in time.

Future Value of $1 The future amount of $1, based on the effects of compound interest.

General Data Information that covers the forces that affect property values but are not directly related to a particular piece of property. General data covers economic, governmental, social and physical factors, and can be local or national.

Gentrification The process of rapid revitalization of properties in a neighborhood, which causes current residents to be displaced.

Government Survey System A legal description for land, referencing principal meridians and base lines designated throughout the country. Also called **Rectangular Survey** or **Township System**.

Grade The slope of land, especially used when discussing land sloping away from the foundation of a structure.

Gross Adjustments The overall total of all adjustments applied regardless of whether the adjustment is applied as a positive or a negative (for example, a +$1,000 and a -$1,000 adjustment would result in $2,000 gross adjustments).

Gross Income Multiplier (GIM) A factor that takes into account income derived from all sources of a property (e.g., vending, storage units). A GIM can be stated as a PGIM or an EGIM.

Gross Lease A property lease where the landlord pays all utilities and expenses.

Gross Living Area (GLA) Residential space that is finished, livable, and above grade. Garages, finished basements, and storage areas usually do not count as GLA.

Gross Rent Multiplier (GRM) A number derived from comparable rental property in an area, which is then used in an income method for indicating a value conclusion.

Ground Fault Interrupter (GFI) A specially grounded outlet that turns off the outlet's power instantaneously if the device or appliance that is plugged in gets wet, shorts out, or malfunctions.

Ground Lease A property lease that only covers the land, often with the lessee owning the building on the land.

Ground Rent The income earned from a ground lease.

Ground Rent Capitalization Method A method of valuing land based on the rent it generates in a given year, divided by an appropriate capitalization rate.

Growth The first stage a neighborhood goes through in its life cycle, when property values rise as development activity begins and continues.

Hard Costs Costs in a project that are not variable, such as labor and materials. Also called **Direct Costs**.

Heat Pump An alternative to traditional heating and cooling systems, whereby one unit provides heat in the winter and cooled air in the summer.

Heating and Cooling System A house system comprised of several elements, including such things as a furnace or heat pump, flue, ducts and ductwork, registers, and thermostat. Also called **HVAC**.

Highest and Best Use The most profitable, legally permitted, economically feasible, and physically possible use of a property.

Home Inspection A visual examination of the physical structure and systems of a home.

Homeowners Association A nonprofit association made up of homeowners in a subdivision, responsible for enforcing the subdivision's CC&Rs and managing other community affairs.

Household A group of people living in one unit of housing.

HUD The Department of Housing and Urban Development; a government agency that deals with housing issues.

HVAC Heating, ventilation, air-conditioning system.

Hypothetical Condition That which is contrary to what exists, but is supposed for the purpose of analysis.

Immobility A physical characteristic of real estate referring to the fact that real estate cannot move from one place to another.

Improvements Additions to real property; they can be natural (e.g., trees or a lot feature), but usually are man-made, substantial fixtures, such as buildings.

Income Money derived from an activity, such as the exertion of labor or investment of capital.

Income Approach An appraisal method that indicates the value of real estate by analyzing the amount of income the property potentially could generate and applying income techniques.

Incurable Something that cannot be fixed at a reasonable cost, with the cost of the repair being more than the value added to a property.

Indestructibility A physical characteristic of real estate referring to the fact that it cannot be destroyed.

Index Method A method for determining the cost of a building by taking its original cost and multiplying that number by an index factor based on how long ago the building was constructed.

Indirect Costs Costs in a project that are variable (costs other than labor or materials) Also called **Soft Costs**.

Inflation An increase in the cost of goods or services; too much money chasing too few goods.

Ingress Means of entry or access to a property.

Insurance Value The amount that the property can be insured for, usually only representing the replacement costs of the structure and disregarding any value for the land.

Intended Use The use or uses of an appraiser's reported appraisal or appraisal review assignment opinions and conclusions, as identified by the appraiser based on communication with the client at the time of the assignment.

Intended User The client and any other party as identified, by name or type, as users of the appraisal or appraisal review report by the appraiser on the basis of communication with the client at the time of the assignment.

Interest 1. A right or share in something, such as a piece of real estate. 2. The charge a borrower pays to a lender for the use of the lender's money.

Interest Rate The cost of money; the additional percentage of a borrowed sum that a borrower must repay to the lender for use of the lender's money.

Interim Use Temporary use of a property while it awaits conversion to its highest and best use (e.g., waiting for a zoning change, accumulation of investment dollars, etc.)

Investment The use of capital designed to produce income and/or profit.

Joist and Rafters (Roofing) A type of roof frame with joists supported by the outer load bearing walls and a central load bearing wall that acts as the beams do for the floor joists. The ceiling joists run horizontally, parallel to the floor; the ceiling rafters begin on the outer load bearing walls, but rise as they come to center peak of the roof.

Joists Long beams of wood or steel that span the piers of a foundation or the load bearing walls of a roof.

Jurisdictional Exception An assignment condition that voids the force of a part or parts of USPAP, when compliance with part or parts of USPAP is contrary to law or public policy applicable to the assignment.

Land The surface of the earth: Actual dirt on the ground, part of a waterway that is owned, or even a swampy marsh. From a legal standpoint, land also refers to everything under the ground to the center of the earth, and everything over the land into the air (within limits to allow for air traffic).

Land Residual Method An income method of site valuation that attributes a certain part of the income produced by a property to the building or other improvement, then attributes the remaining income to the land.

Land Use Controls Public or private restrictions on how land may be used.

Landlocked Property 1. Land without access to a road or highway. 2. Land not beside water.

Landlord A landowner who has leased his property to another. Also called **lessor**.

Latent Defect A defect that is not visible or apparent; a hidden defect that would not be discovered in a reasonably thorough inspection of property.

Lease Conveyance of a leasehold estate from the fee owner to a tenant; a contract where one party pays the other rent in exchange for possession of real estate.

Lease/Option When a seller leases property to someone for a specific term, with an option to buy the property at a predetermined price during the term. Usually, a portion of the lease payments is applied to the purchase price.

Leased Fee Estate The landlord's ownership interest in leased property.

Leasehold Estate An estate that gives the holder (tenant) a temporary right to possession, without title.

Legal Description A precise description of a parcel of property.

Legally Permissible A use of land available to the owner under current laws and zoning regulations.

Lessee A person who leases property; a tenant.

Lessor A person who leases property to another; a landlord.

Levy 1. Verb: To impose a tax. 2. Noun: The tax itself.

License 1. Official permission to do a particular thing that the law does not allow everyone to do. 2. Revocable, non-assignable permission to enter another person's land for a particular purpose.

Lien 1. A non-possessory interest in property, giving a lienholder the right to foreclose if the owner does not pay a debt owed to lienholder. 2. A financial encumbrance on the owner's title.

Lien, General A lien against all property of a debtor, instead of a particular piece of property.

Lien, Involuntary A lien that arises by operation of law, without the consent of the property owner. Also called **Statutory Lien**.

Life Estate A freehold estate that lasts only as long as a specified person lives. That person is referred to as the **life tenant** or **measuring life**.

Life Tenant Someone who owns a life estate; the person entitled to possession of the property during the measuring life.

Limiting Conditions Statement by the appraiser explaining the framework used to reach the appraisal value and establishing the report's limitations.

Linkages The proximity of property to common destinations and conveniences, and the time required to reach those places.

Littoral Rights The water rights of a landowner whose property is adjacent to a lake or contains a lake; also called **Riparian Rights**, although that term literally refers only to the water rights of a landowner on a river.

Loan-to-Value Ratio (LTV) The loan amount compared to the market value of the property.

Location The exact position of real estate.

Location Survey The process of verifying that an improvement properly sits within the boundaries of the property and there are no encroachments from neighboring land onto the subject property.

Long-lived Item A component of the property that is not expected to be replaced during the life of a property.

Lot A parcel of land; especially, a parcel in a subdivision.

Lot and Block A legal description used for platted property. The description states only the property's lot and block number in a particular subdivision; to find out the exact location of property boundaries, the plat map for that subdivision must be consulted at the county recorder's office.

Macroeconomic Economic elements that affect the entire market.

Management Fee Money collected by an individual or company for overseeing a project, rental properties, etc.

Market Place where goods are exchanged, often between buyers and sellers.

Market Analysis A study of supply and demand, as well as other economic conditions in an area. Also called **Market Study**.

Market Area The broadest of all terms identifying the boundaries of a particular area. Market area takes into account the land uses and characteristics of typical market participants within the defined area.

Market Price The price that property sold for in an actual transaction.

Market Rent What the property could rent for in the open market if it were currently vacant and available.

Market Study A study of supply and demand, as well as other economic conditions in an area. Also called **Market Analysis**.

Market Value Generally, the most probable price that a property should bring in a competitive and open market. There could be many definitions. The appraiser must always identify the definition of market value and cite its source in the report.

Marketability The ability of a product to attract buyers.

Marketability Study Analysis of the likelihood that a particular product will sell.

Marketable Title Title free and clear of objectionable encumbrances or defects, so that a reasonably prudent person with full knowledge of the facts would not hesitate to purchase the property.

Mass Appraisal The process of valuing a universe of properties (more than one) as of a given date using standard methodology, employing common data, and allowing for statistical testing.

Matched Pair Analysis Process of determining the value of specific property characteristics or features by comparing pairs of similar properties. Also called **Paired Data Analysis**.

Metes and Bounds Description A legal description that starts at an easily identifiable point of beginning (POB), then describes the property's boundaries in terms of courses (compass directions) and distances, ultimately returning to the POB.

Microeconomic Economic elements that affect a narrow portion of the market.

Mineral Rights Rights to the minerals located beneath the surface of a property.

Modified Age-Life Method A combination of the age-life method and the breakdown method of depreciation. This method can be employed when curable depreciation is attributable to obsolescence for which the depreciation can be readily recognized and calculated.

Monetary Policy The means by which the government can exert control over the supply and cost of money.

Monuments Fixed physical objects used in a metes and bounds description as points of reference. Also called **Markers**.

Mortgage An instrument that pledges and creates a voluntary lien on real property to secure repayment of a debt. The parties to a mortgage are the mortgagor (borrower) and mortgagee (lender).

Mortgage, Construction A temporary loan used to finance the construction of a building on land. Replaced with a takeout loan.

Mortgage, Purchase Money A mortgage for which the seller finances all or part of the sale price of a piece of property.

Mortgage Constant The ratio between annual debt service and loan principal.

Mortgagee A lender who accepts a mortgage as security for repayment of the loan.

Mortgagor The borrower in a loan who gives a mortgage to the lender as security.

Most Profitable Use The use of a property that will maximize the owner's capital investment.

Multiple Listing Service (MLS) A listing service whereby local member brokers agree to share listings, and agree to share commissions on properties sold jointly.

Multiple Regression Analysis Statistical measure that attempts to ascertain the source of change in multiple variables.

Multiple Use Property A property that has a limited number of unique uses that may or may not be used simultaneously or with little modification to the property. Also called **Multiple Purpose Property**.

Neighborhood A compilation of complementary land uses.

Net Adjustments The sum of the adjustments taking into account whether the adjustment was a positive or a negative. (For example, a +$1,000 and a -$1,000 adjustment would result in $0 net adjustments.)

Net Household Formations The number of new households being formed or moving into the area, minus the number of households leaving the area.

Net Lease A property lease where the tenant pays some or all utilities and expenses, in addition to rent payments.

Net Operating Income (NOI) Income after expenses.

Non-Conforming Use Property use that does not conform to current zoning laws, but is allowed because the property was being used that way before the new zoning law was passed.

Non-Possessory Interest 1. An interest in property that does not include the right to possess and occupy the property. 2. An encumbrance, such as a lien or easement.

Nuisance Anything outside property boundaries that interferes with the right of quiet enjoyment.

Observable Depreciation Method of determining depreciation based on inspection of the structure, study of demographics, and analysis of the market or other external conditions.

Obsolescence A loss in value because of inherent design flaws or other defects not easily corrected.

Operating Expenses Day-to-day costs of running a building, such as repairs and maintenance, but not including debt service or depreciation.

Opportunity Cost The loss in value or potential value that occurs because one action is chosen over another.

Ordinance A law passed by a local legislative body, such as a city or village council.

Overimprovement An improvement that exceeds the highest and best use for the site and does not increase the value of the real property in proportion to its cost.

Ownership Title to and dominion over property; the rights of possession and control of real or personal property.

Parcel A lot or tract of real estate, particularly a specified part of a larger tract.

Partial Interest Any interest in real estate that one may have, other than full bundle of rights.

Party Wall A wall built along the boundary line between two parcels of land, where part of the wall rests on each side.

Patent Defect A visible, apparent defect that can be seen in a reasonably thorough inspection of property.

Percentage Adjustments Adjustment applied to the sale price of a comparable sale whereby the appraiser translates a dollar figure from a paired-data analysis into a percentage change in value.

Percentage Lease A type of lease that requires the lessee to make rental payments based (either in whole or in part) on a percentage of the gross sales, net sales, income, profit or some other value.

Percentage Rent Lease payment that is based on the sales of the tenant, with the landlord receiving a percentage of the tenant's sales, often in addition to a minimum rent amount.

Permits Official government documents that acknowledge work that a person wants to do on a property and allow it to be done.

Personal Property 1. Tangible items not permanently attached to or part of real estate. 2. Any property that is not real property. 3. Movable property not affixed to land. Also called **Chattel** or **Personalty**.

Personalty Personal property.

Physical Characteristics Indestructibility-Immobility-Uniqueness-Scarcity; the four physical characteristics of real estate.

Physical Deterioration Wear and tear on something due to age, the elements, or other forces.

Pin A rod driven into the ground to serve as a marker for a metes and bounds legal description.

Pitch A roof's vertical rise in inches, divided by its horizontal span in feet.

Planned Unit Development (PUD) A special type of subdivision that may combine nonresidential uses with residential uses, or otherwise depart from ordinary zoning and subdivision regulations; some PUDs have lot owners co-own recreational facilities or open spaces as tenants in common.

Planning Commission A local government agency responsible for preparing a community's comprehensive development plan.

Plans and Specifications Construction blueprints.

Plat A detailed survey map of a subdivision or other grouped lots of land, recorded in the county where the land is located. Subdivided property is often called **Platted Property**. Also called **Plat Map**.

Plat Book A large book containing subdivision plats, kept at the county recorder's office.

Platform (Framing) A type of framing used to build a house or building one story at a time, with each story serving as a platform for the next story to be built.

Plot Plan A drawing showing the layout of the subject site, including the positioning of the improvements. Also called **Plot Map**.

Plottage Is realized as an increase in value when two or more parcels are assembled.

Plumbing System A house system comprised of several elements including piping, drains, clean outs, vents, valves, faucets, sinks, toilets, tubs, showers, and hot water tank. Gas lines may also be included.

Point of Beginning (POB) The starting and ending point for a metes and bounds description. Also called **Point of Origin**.

Points One percent of a loan amount. Points can be charged for any reason, but often are used for buydowns. Also called **Discount Points**.

Police Power The constitutional power of state and local governments to enact and enforce laws that protect the public's health, safety, morals, and general welfare.

Possession 1. Holding and enjoying property. 2. Actual physical occupation of real property.

Possessory Interest An interest in property that entitles the holder to possess and occupy the property, now or in the future; an estate, which may be either a freehold or leasehold.

Post and Beam (Framing) A type of framing with the floor for higher stories (and the roof) supported by beams that sit on top of posts and the outside wall perimeter.

Potential Gross Income (PGI) The income that could be produced by a property in an ideal situation, with no vacancy or collection losses.

Present Value of $1 The value today of an amount that will be received in the future, based on the effects of compound interest.

Price The amount asked, offered, or paid for a property. *

Principal Meridians Main north-south lines designated and named throughout the country for use with the government survey system.

Productivity Analysis A means of determining the current position of a property in relation to the marketplace. Also called **Property Productivity Analysis** or **Productivity Market Analysis**.

Progression A principle that says the value of a home is helped by the other homes in an area. Usually said about the "worst" home in the "best" area.

Property 1. The rights of ownership in a thing, such as the right to use, possess, transfer, or encumber real estate. 2. Something that is owned, real or personal.

Public Record The official collection of legal documents that individuals have filed with the county recorder to make the information contained in them public.

Purchase Ability The prospective buyer having enough disposable income available to satisfy his or her needs, wants, and desires. Also called **Effective Demand** or **Effective Purchasing Power**.

Purchase Agreement A contract in which a seller promises to convey title to real property to a buyer in exchange for the purchase price.

Purpose of the Appraisal A statement of the type of value defined in an assignment.

Quantity Survey Method A cost approach appraisal method in which the appraiser counts the number and type of each part and material used to construct the building, adding costs for labor, profit, permits, etc.

Quiet Enjoyment Use and possession of real property without interference from a previous owner, the lessor, or anyone else claiming title.

Radon Gas A naturally occurring radioactive gas that emanates from the earth; it is odorless, colorless, and tasteless but has been identified as a cancer-causing agent.

Rafters Sloped support beams that follow the pitch of the roof and serve to hold the outer roof covering.

Range Lines In the government survey system, north-south lines that run parallel to principal meridians at six-mile intervals.

Real Estate The actual physical land and everything, both natural and man-made, attached (or appurtenant) to it.

Real Estate Contract 1. A purchase agreement. 2. A land contract. 3. Any contract having to do with real property.

Real Estate Cycles General swings in real estate activity, resulting in increasing or decreasing activity and property values during different phases of the cycle.

Real Property Not only the physical land and everything attached to it, but also the rights of ownership in the real estate. Also called **Realty**.

Realty Real property.

Reconciliation Analyzing the values derived from the different appraisal approaches to arrive at a final opinion of value.

Recording Filing a document at the county recorder's office, so it will be placed in the public record.

Regression A principle that says the value of a home is held down by the other homes in an area. Usually said about the "best" home in the "worst" area.

Regression Analysis Statistical measure that attempts to ascertain the source of change in variables.

Regulation 1. A rule adopted by an administrative agency. 2. Any governmental order having the force of law.

Release 1. To give up a legal right. 2. A document in which a legal right is given up.

Remaining Economic Life The period of usefulness that a building has remaining as of the effective date of the appraisal.

Rent Consideration paid by tenant to landlord in exchange for possession and use of property.

Replacement Cost The estimated cost new of building the functional equivalent (substitute) of the original structure, using modern materials and workmanship and current-day standards of size, layout, quality, and utility.

Report Any communication, written or oral, of an appraisal or appraisal review that is transmitted to the client upon completion of an assignment.

Reproduction Cost The estimated cost new of replicating the original building, using identical materials, workmanship, construction standards, size, layout, quality, and utility that is present in the current structure;

including any functional obsolescence, deficiencies, and superadequacies.

Reserves for Replacement An amount of money set aside for future replacement of major items, such as the roof or heating system. Also called **Reserves**.

Restriction A limitation on the use of real property.

Restriction, Deed Limitations on real property use, imposed through language included in the deed.

Restriction, Private Restriction imposed on property by a previous owner or subdivision developer.

Restriction, Public A law or regulation limiting or regulating the use of real property, such as zoning.

Restrictive Covenant 1. A limitation on real property use, imposed by a former owner. 2. A promise to do or not do an act relating to real property, usually the owner's promise to not use property in a particular way. Cannot caused forfeiture of title.

Revenue Generating Laws Laws enacted by government consisting of taxation and specific tax policies.

Revitalization The final stage a neighborhood goes through in its life cycle, when property values rise again as demand increases, resulting in increased renovation and rehabilitation.

Right of Disposal A right to transfer all or some of a person's ownership interest in real property.

Right of Enjoyment A right to enjoy the benefits of land ownership without outside interference.

Right of Use Right of land ownership to make it productive. Part of the bundle of rights.

Right of Way An easement giving the holder the right to cross another person's land.

Right to Regulate Laws Laws enacted by governments dealing with the police power they reserve for themselves.

Riparian Rights The water rights of a landowner whose property is adjacent to or crossed by a river.

Rough-Ins Any type of interior work to a house or building that is not part of the finish work.

Sales Comparison Approach An appraisal method that indicates the value of real property by comparing the property being appraised with other comparable properties. Data are collected and adjustments are made for differences. Also called **Market Approach** or **Sales Comparison Method**.

Scarcity A physical characteristic of real property that says there is a limited supply of real estate; the perceived supply of a good or service relative to the demand for the item.

Scope of Work The type and extent of research and analyses in an appraisal or appraisal review assignment.

Section Part of a township, one-mile by one-mile square, used for the government survey system; one section equals 640 acres, 36 sections equal one township.

Segmentation A process that involves identifying and categorizing the various sub-markets that exist within a larger market, focusing on participants on the demand side of the market.

Seller Financing When a seller extends credit to a buyer to finance the purchase of the property; this can happen instead of or in addition to the buyer obtaining a loan from a third party, such as an institutional lender.

Seller's Market A situation in the real estate market where sellers can choose from a large number of buyers looking for property in an area.

Service Companies The companies in an area that serve the needs of the base companies, base industries, and their employees.

Setback Requirements Provisions in a zoning ordinance that do not allow structures to be built within a certain distance of property lines.

Short-Lived Item A component of the property that is expected to be replaced during the life of a property.

Single Use Property A property that is specifically designed and/or built for the user, or one with a unique use that would likely not fit other users.

Sinking Fund An account in which money is deposited and allowed to accumulate to cover a future expense.

Site A parcel of land with enhancements that make it ready for a building or structure.

Situs A term used to describe the place where something exists, an area of preference, or preference by people for a certain location.

Soft Costs Costs in a project that are variable (costs other than labor or materials) Also called **Indirect Costs**.

Special Assessment A tax levied only against properties that benefit from a public improvement (e.g., a sewer or street light), to cover the cost of the improvement; this creates a **special assessment lien**, an involuntary lien.

Special Use Property A property that has limited and specific uses, such as a church. Also called **Special Purpose Property**.

Specific Data Information that is relevant to the subject property itself. Two types of specific data are **subject property data** and **comparative purpose data**.

Stability The second stage a neighborhood goes through in its life cycle, when the area is built up to the point where there is little, if any, vacant property. Also called **Equilibrium**.

Standard Deviation Statistical measure that calculates the variation from the mean. Describes the dispersion of a population or sample in a data set.

Standing Seam—A type of roof, usually made from metal.

Standing Stock Completed construction projects (e.g., houses) that have not yet been sold.

State Implementation Plan (SIP) A study required by Federal Environmental Protection Agency to help states meet national air quality standards.

Statute A law enacted by a state legislature or the U.S. Congress.

Stigmatized Property A property made undesirable to most people by a past event, often a crime or environmental hazard.

Subdivision 1. A piece of land divided into two or more parcels. 2. A residential development.

Subdivision Analysis Method A method of valuing land that could be developed, by taking the total projected market value of the finished project and subtracting all costs of development and entrepreneurial profit and incentive.

Sublease When a tenant transfers only part of his or her right of possession or other interest in leased property to another for part of the remaining lease term (as opposed to an assignment, where the tenant gives up possession for the remainder of the lease term).

Sub-Markets A subset of the larger real estate market.

Substitution A principle that says an informed buyer will not pay more for a property, or a feature in a property, than a comparable substitute.

Substructure The area of a structure that is below grade.

Superadequacy A feature of an improvement that is more than is necessary for the operation of the improvement.

Superstructure The area of a structure that is above grade.

Supply and Demand A principle of economics that says, for all products, goods and services, when supply exceeds demand, prices will fall and when demand exceeds supply, prices will rise.

Support, Lateral The support that land receives from the land adjacent to it.

Support, Subjacent The support that the surface of land receives from the land beneath it.

Support Rights The right to have one's land supported by land adjacent to and beneath it.

Surplus Site The portion over and above what is necessary for the highest and best use of the subject property, and does not have a stand-alone highest and best use. Surplus land is not needed to expand the subject improvements or that of an adjoining property.

Survey The process of locating and measuring the boundaries of a property, and identifying the improvements, encroachments, and easements associated with that land.

Taking When the government acquires private property for public use by appropriation, it is called a taking. The term is also used in inverse condemnation lawsuits, when a government action has made private property useless.

Tangible Property Items that can be held or touched (usually personal property).

Tax, Property An annual tax levied on the value of real property.

Taxation The process of a government levying a charge on people or things

Tear-down Properties When properties are worth less than the underlying land, and thus, people are willing to incur the costs of tearing down the present structure to use the land.

Tenant Someone in lawful possession of real property, especially someone who has leased property from the owner.

Timeshare Property ownership where several people own the property, or the right to possess it, and agree to use it at different intervals.

Title Actual lawful ownership of real property. Title is not a document. Title is a *concept*.

Topography The physical characteristics of the surface of a parcel of land.

Township Square divisions of land, 6 miles by 6 miles, in the government survey system. One township contains 36 sections.. Two common types of traps are **S-Traps** and **P-Traps**.

Transferability The ability to freely buy, sell, encumber, or dispose of property in any way the owner sees fit.

Trespass An unlawful physical invasion of property owned by another.

Underimprovement When the improvements do not conform to the highest and best use of the site, thus the property does not achieve maximum value.

Uniform Residential Appraisal Report (URAR) A standard appraisal report form used by lenders and appraisers because it has been developed and approved by secondary mortgage market participants Fannie Mae and Freddie Mac.

Uniform Standards of Professional Appraisal Practice (USPAP) Professional appraisal standards promulgated by The Appraisal Foundation, and widely recognized throughout the United States as accepted standards of appraisal practice.

Uniqueness A physical characteristic of real property that says that each piece of land, each building, and each house is a different piece of real estate. Also called **Non-homogeneity**.

Unit-In-Place Method A method for determining the cost of a building that estimates the cost of reproducing it, by determining the unit cost of each of the component parts of the structure and adding them together based on actual need and usage.

Urea-Formaldehyde Foam Insulation A type of insulation popular at one point because it could be blown into an existing structure. It is now banned for home use by the EPA due to potential health risks from its toxic fumes.

Useful Life The period of time a structure or a component of the structure can be expected to function for the purpose it was designed for and relates only to physical deterioration.

Utility The ability of a good or service to satisfy human wants, needs, or desires.

Vacancy and Collection Losses Estimate of how much future income may be lost when a building is not full or tenants fail to pay the rent.

Valuation Services Services that pertain to different aspects of property valuation. Valuation services are provided by appraisers and those in other professions.

Value The amount of goods or services offered in the marketplace in exchange for something else.

Value in Use The value of property to the owner as it is presently being utilized, without considering highest and best use or present market value (e.g., the value that property actually contributes to the owner's business).

Value, Assessed The value placed on property by a taxing authority for the purposes of taxation. With real estate, this value is usually a fraction of true value.

Value, Book The value of property as capital, based on accounting methods.

Value, Insurance The amount that property can be insured for, usually only representing the replacement costs of the structure and disregarding any value for the land.

Value, Liquidation The value a property could get if sold under duress or in a must-sell situation with less than typical market exposure.

Value, Loan The amount of money a lender is willing to loan to someone to finance a particular piece of property.

Value, Market Generally, the most probable price that a property should bring in a competitive and open market. There could be many definitions. The appraiser must always identify the definition of market value and cite its source in the report

Value, Salvage Value of a property's useful components that can be removed before demolition.

Variable Expenses Operating expenses necessary to the property, but dependent on the property's occupancy level.

Variance A permit obtained from the local zoning authority allowing the holder to use property or build a structure in a way that violates the zoning ordinance.

Variance, Area A variance that permits a property owner to bend the rules regarding building size, height limits, setbacks, side yards, parking, etc.

Variance, Use A variance that permits a property owner to use land in a way that's not allowed in that zone—such as commercial use in a residential zone.

Vaulted Ceiling A type of ceiling that rises as it follows the roof line, extending to the roof peak. Also called a **Cathedral Ceiling**.

Veteran's Administration (VA) The government agency that guarantees mortgage loans for eligible veterans.

Waste Destruction, damage, or material alteration of property by someone in possession who holds less than a fee estate, such as a life tenant or lessee.

Water Rights The right to use water in or from a river, stream, or lake.

Weighted Average A statistical method that gives more importance to certain results.

Workfile The documentation necessary to support the appraiser's analyses, opinions, and conclusions.

Yield The total amount of money that can be made from an investment.

Zoning Government regulation of the uses of property within specified areas.

Zoning, Down When tighter restrictions are placed on land usage in a given area. The primary way this is done is by changing zoning laws with regard to building density or setback requirement to allow fewer buildings.

Zoning, Exclusionary A zoning law that effectively prevents certain groups (e.g., minorities, people with lower income) from living in a community.

Zoning, Pass-Through When zoning laws are set up in a hierarchical fashion, such that all uses above the current zoning are permitted.

Zoning, Spot An illegal rezone that favors (or restricts) a particular property owner (or a small group of owners) without justification.

Zoning Laws Local ordinances dividing a city, county, etc., into zones, specifying different types of land use in different areas. This is a type of government restriction via police power.

*2014-2015 USPAP DEFINITIONS

Index

R

S

T

U

V

Z